Mentoring in Action

A Month-by-Month Curriculum for Mentors and Their New Teachers

Carol Pelletier

Boston College

Boston • New York • San Francisco
Mexico City • Montreal • Toronto • London • Madrid • Munich • Paris
Hong Kong • Singapore • Tokyo • Cape Town • Sydney

Executive Editor and Publisher: Stephen D. Dragin
Series Editorial Assistant: Meaghan Minnick
Marketing Manager: Tara Kelly
Production Editor: Greg Erb
Editorial Production Service: Walsh & Associates, Inc.
Manufacturing and Composition Buyer: Andrew Turso
Interior Design and Electronic Composition: Denise Hoffman
Cover Designer: Kristina Mose-Libon

For related titles and support materials, visit our online catalog at www.ablongman.com.

Between the time Web site information is gathered and then published, it is not unusual for some sites to have closed. Also, the transcription of URLs can result in unintended typographical errors. The publisher would appreciate notification where these errors occur so that they may be corrected in subsequent editions.

ISBN: 0-205-43898-9. Cataloging-in-Publication Data unavailable at press time.

Printed in the United States of America

10 9 8 7 6 5 4 3 2 1 VHP 10 09 08 07 06 05

Contents

August

September

January

Beginning a New Calendar Year: Looking Back and Moving Forward 135

February

Engaging Students in the Curriculum: Focus on Content through Active Inquiry 157

Preface

This book is an assimilation of work that first began with a mentoring course I co-taught with Lee Teitel, a collaborative, enthusiastic professor at the University of Massachusetts Boston. I am inspired by the many conversations I have had over the years with both experienced and new teachers, and I developed this guide for them. Since there are many existing books for mentors and new teachers on the market today, I wanted to add to the knowledge base in a new way. We have to acknowledge the fact that busy teachers need space and time to mentor, and it has to fit into the month-by-month curriculum that already exists in schools. This guide recognizes that mentors are essential to the induction process, but I believe they do need curriculum maps to carry out their mentoring work. My hope is that this guide will provide curriculum topics and structure that will allow mentoring conversations to happen throughout the school year.

Special thanks to Steve Dragin at Pearson Education for believing in me and giving me this opportunity to contribute to the mentoring discussion.

I dedicate this book to my husband, David,
a wonderfully creative writer.

Introduction

Dear Mentors and District Induction Coordinators,

Mentoring new teachers is an exciting and rewarding experience. You will not only have an opportunity to share your expertise, but you will also add to it by learning from the new teachers. This generation of new teachers brings vitality, idealism, and some excellent computer skills with them. Mentors and school districts need all of these today! Wherever you are in the process of teacher induction, whether it is designing the vision, providing workshops to new teachers, or evaluating what you have done successfully, I am glad you are considering this curriculum as one way to guide you.

This book suggests that mentors can be facilitators of small groups of new teachers. Mentors can go beyond the one-on-one conversations in a dyad with one mentor and one new teacher to a collegial group where all members, including the mentor, participate and learn. This curriculum relies on the expertise of the experienced teacher as a mentor/facilitator, but recognizes that one mentor cannot know all things and be all things for any new teacher. This collaborative approach allows everyone in the group to share ideas, issues, and solutions to problems. Not only does it take the pressure off the mentor, it enriches the discussions. If you find yourself working with only one new teacher, you can invite others in the school to take part in some of your discussions during the school year.

Why Induction?

We all agree that systematically inducting new teachers into the profession with mentoring support as part of induction works. Research has been done to prove it, and common sense tells us that it is the right thing to do with new teachers. We know that the "sink or swim" method of induction doesn't provide support. Who wouldn't want a mentor during the most stressful time in his or her career? So if we agree that induction and mentoring works, what's the problem?

What I have discovered in informal conversations with mentors from all over the United States is that we are facing similar issues. Some districts don't have enough mentors for one-on-one mentoring, other districts don't have mentors in close proximity to the new teachers, and still others don't have any release time to facilitate conversations between a mentor and a new teacher if they do have mentors. More time is spent "matching" than is spent on the actual content of the discussions. Some mentors are assigned and don't know what they should do with the new teacher. There is no curriculum for mentoring discussions.

We also know that new teachers are not staying in teaching. We are doing a great job recruiting and hiring, but they still are finding their way out of teaching during the first three to five years. Induction programs are inconsistent, and underfunded, and mentors have little preparation or support while they are in the process of mentoring. These barriers of funding, time, training, support, and release time impact the quality of the induction program and may be impacting the retention rate for new teachers.

Why This Book?

My hope is that this book will provide a common language and a curriculum that mentors can use to frame discussions with new teachers. It is not the "be all" book, but rather just one small part of an enormously complex task of induction. It is designed to be used with small groups of new teachers, allowing a district with a few mentors a viable mentoring option. Although the curriculum discussions will be richer with small groups, they certainly can be successful in a one-on-one mentoring model. The key component to the book is the structure for weekly and monthly meetings that offer a variety of possible topics to discuss. It responds to a common question mentors often ask, "What are we supposed to talk about every week?"

By using the Interstate New Teacher Assessment and Support Consortium (INTASC) Principles in each chapter, you will have a common language of standards. There are quotes from students of all ages and comments from new teachers in their first year of teaching that help maintain the spirit of both teaching and learning each month. The curriculum guide is organized by months because that is what mentors who talked to me said they wanted. For schools on year-round schedules, I invite you to modify the months and make the book work for you.

Why Now?

Districts need this type of book now because so many new teachers are entering teaching. Some enter through traditional pathways and others by alternative routes. Mentors may have to differentiate their mentoring based on the needs of the new teachers with whom they will be working. This guide may become a review for new teachers who come to you well prepared by Colleges of Education. Use it to promote teacher leadership among them. We know we need more new, young teachers in our schools. New teachers who have entered teaching through alternative routes may need this in-depth mentoring because they did not participate in student teaching or did not have the benefit of pedagogy. You may need to use this text as a teacher preparation guide for them.

Why Me?

I have a passion for this work. I have been a teacher and a teacher educator for 33 years, 21 years in a public school and 12 years as the Director of Practicum Experiences. Recently I added the role of Teacher Induction to my work. Following the Boston College graduates into their first years of teaching has been rewarding and eye opening. My first question was, "How can I support our new teachers when they are in so many different social contexts?"

During my visits to schools, my talks with mentors led me to create this book for mentors like you. All the mentors I talked with wanted to mentor a new teacher, they just didn't know exactly what they were supposed to be doing all the time. They also asked me for suggestions and ways to mentor when they didn't have any release time. These dedicated professionals, like you, who gave up their time to nurture, challenge, and support new teachers, wanted some help. This book is a result of those many conversations. They will be happy to see that the five-, ten-, fifteen-, and twenty-minute meetings are in the Appendix of this book. I have learned that you can do something with a new teacher in five minutes if you have it planned, and it can make a difference.

Will this book make a difference in teacher retention? We won't know that for sure. Certainly we need to carefully research the area of teacher induction and mentoring. What is possible is that meeting with new teachers and using a mentoring curriculum may add to the effectiveness of your school and district induction program.

Why You?

Why did you say yes to mentor a new teacher or coordinate a district program? How will you contribute and share your expertise while you honor the expertise of these new teachers?

I hope you will find inspiration and motivation in the pages of this book to support you in your work with new teachers. Use their positive energy and vitality to sustain you as you guide the next generation of teachers into this noble profession.

Sincerely,

Carol Pelletier

Dr. Carol Pelletier
Director of Practicum Experiences & Teacher Induction
Boston College

Part I Inducting a New Teacher into the Teaching Profession

Schools and districts are expected to provide high-quality induction for the new teachers who are entering the teaching profession because retaining high-quality teachers has become a priority in the United States. Research is showing that more than 50 percent of new teachers hired are leaving before their fifth year of teaching. Researchers are asking why and getting a variety of responses. Induction programs are faced with supporting new teachers who have entered into high-need teaching positions through alternative routes who have no teaching pedagogy. The need for release time, resources for meetings and professional development, and well-prepared mentors continues to challenge districts. Mentoring and induction are used interchangeably, and the terms confuse new teachers, district coordinators, and mentors. So what is induction?

Components of a High-Quality Induction Program

What Is Induction?

If you ask different people, you will get different answers because there are several ways to define induction. *Induction* is defined in Merriam-Webster as "1a: the act or process of inducting (as into office); b: an initial experience; c: the formality by which a civilian is inducted into military service." Most people think of military induction (c:). Many teachers don't like the term induction for that reason and prefer to use "mentoring" instead. This leads to confusion about what induction actually is, because mentoring is just one of the components of an effective induction program.

We would agree then that b: an initial experience applies to new teachers who are entering teaching for the very first time. New teachers will have an "initial experience" by nature of just being in teaching in that first year. Whether the experience is positive or negative is another question. "An initial experience" still doesn't describe what induction actually is. Many articles have been written on induction and mentoring; in my opinion the leader in the area of teacher induction is the New Teacher Center at the University of Santa Cruz in California. This

Center has been developing models for new teachers and mentors for almost two decades and serves as a model for both research and practice. While it offers all of us practical ideas, inspiration, and research-based studies to improve the work of induction, its leader, Ellen Moir, continues to expand the vision to bring more teachers the induction support they need to survive in twenty-first-century classrooms.

Based on my reading and talking and interacting with school districts, I believe we need several key components to create successful high-quality induction programs. You may add your own, but the lesson here is that there are several components to induction, and it is not just mentoring. The components I suggest are a clear plan for the program, resources, orientations throughout the school year, mentoring (one-on-one or small groups), professional development, and a program evaluation to see if teachers actually felt supported by the program. The larger research question is, "Do they stay in teaching?"

A Plan for Induction

Districts may have an induction committee or advisory board to design what the new teachers entering the district may need to be successful. Induction should go beyond the first year because it takes several years to "become" a teacher. Some teachers and researchers say that teachers hit their stride in their tenth year. That's a lot of induction to get to the place of effectiveness. Most districts concentrate on the first year of teaching because it is the most stressful one for the new teachers. If you have an opportunity to be part of the induction committee, try to stretch the vision beyond year one. The committee may also want to induct teachers who are new to the system, but have taught before, or who are new to a grade level. This differentiated induction requires resources and different guiding principles because these teachers will have some experience and may not require or need all of the components listed here.

The key to planning induction is to set goals and design the evaluation at the same time. This is the "big picture" plan for the program. Sometimes it is helpful to draw it out first. What do you want the induction program to do? How many years will you support new teachers? How will you be able to measure the results of what you do? How will you define success? Who should be included in designing the plan (second year teachers, other teachers, mentors)? Write the goals and refer to them during the year. Make them public so everyone in the school knows what induction means and how it is different from mentoring.

Resources

It costs money to organize an induction program. Several states have mandated school districts to provide induction and mentoring, but they have not funded these mandates. Unfunded mandates cause financial pressure in districts because the money has to be taken from other internal budgets. Schools need all their resources for teaching students and are challenged to stretch the finances further, so induction and mentoring sometimes are limited to paper plans with little real implementation. Finding creative ways to fund teacher induction programs is challenging. Time is money. Time to release mentors or new teachers to observe each other costs the districts substitute money. Materials and training cost money. We need to lobby to get these mandates funded and in the meantime think of creative ways to assist the new teachers in their initial experience in teaching. A complex and challenging issue to be sure!

Orientations

As new teachers begin their teaching, they have lots of nuts-and-bolts-type questions. These can be served through orientations. Districts who may have financial resources may use their district mentors to also orient the new teachers to the school and the district. Most districts do this as large-group meetings with small breakouts by school or department. These orientations are important because they relate to the survival needs of the teachers. Where do I do the copying? Where do I pick up my paycheck? The mistake most districts make is that the

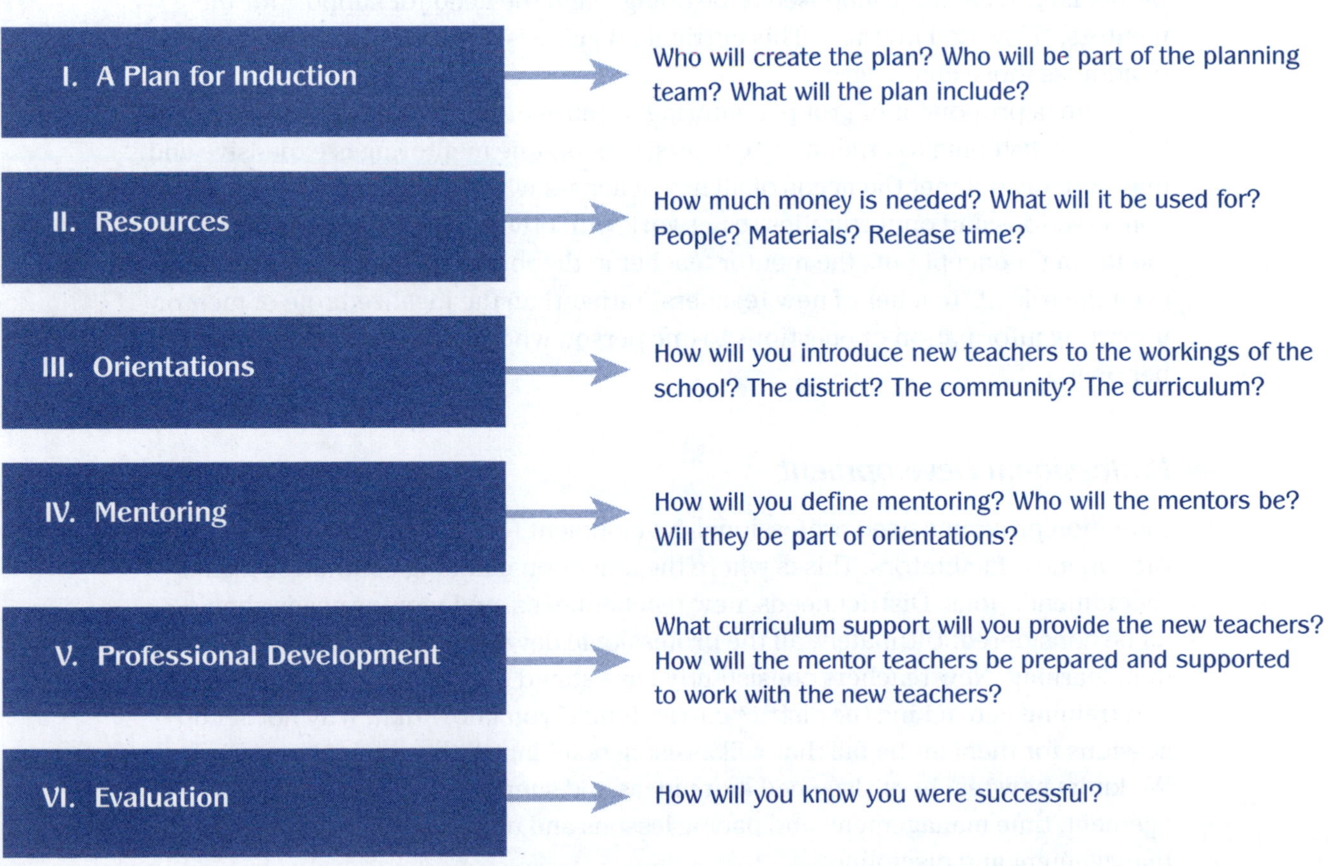
Components of a High Quality Induction Program
I. A Plan for Induction
Who will create the plan? Who will be part of the planning team? What will the plan include?
II. Resources
How much money is needed? What will it be used for? People? Materials? Release time?
III. Orientations
How will you introduce new teachers to the workings of the school? The district? The community? The curriculum?
IV. Mentoring
How will you define mentoring? Who will the mentors be? Will they be part of orientations?
V. Professional Development
What curriculum support will you provide the new teachers? How will the mentor teachers be prepared and supported to work with the new teachers?
VI. Evaluation
How will you know you were successful?

orientations are only held in August as if all the new things that happen to a new teacher happen in the beginning of the school year. An effective induction program will have orientations throughout the school year, especially toward the end of the year to assist in closing out the room (see June in Part II).

Orientations also may include ways to "navigate school culture" in both the school and the district. New teachers don't know who sits in which chair in the teachers' room. They don't know that students are supposed to walk to the buses on the left side of the hallway. They don't know that you have to bring your students to the art room five minutes early. These "culture" issues often cause a great deal of distress for new teachers who have no social relationships or history in this school. Some of these issues can be part of the mentoring conversations as well, depending upon the sensitive nature of the issue.

Mentoring

The entire induction program is most often thought of as assigning a mentor to a new teacher—perhaps because that is all the district can afford, perhaps because there is little understanding of the variety of components of induction, or perhaps because that is the choice of the district. Having the mentor as the sole provider of support for the new teacher puts enormous pressure on one person who is usually teaching full time. The issues that arise with mentors relate to the need for preparation, i.e., "What am I supposed to be doing?" and the need for support for the mentors, "How do I do this?" This curriculum guide is one tool that could be used to address those challenges.

I am a proponent of group mentoring because in my experience new teachers benefit by listening to other new teachers. One-on-one mentoring is expensive and may actually not met the needs of all new teachers who are looking for interactive conversations and opportunities to network with other new teachers. This "group mentoring" concept puts the mentor teacher in the role of facilitator and perhaps even the role of "teacher of new teachers" rather than the idealized role of mentor imparting information or questions to one person who solves them on his or her own.

Professional Development

Induction programs need professional development for both the new teachers and their mentor/facilitators. This is where the induction planning committee makes recommendations. District needs, new teacher needs, and mentor needs should all be considered. Ultimately, all the professional development will relate to student learning. New teachers consistently have stated they need more information and training in teaching the district curriculum. If you know that, why not set up sessions for them in the fall that will assist in teaching all the curriculum areas? We know new teachers also need more ideas and support with classroom management, time management, and pacing lessons and units, as well as behavior management and discipline.

These workshops could be hosted by classroom teachers in their own classrooms, or they could be led by outside consultants. If an outside vendor is contracted for the district, remember that the new teachers need to be in their own groups by grade level because their needs will be very different from experienced teachers. Another approach is to have teachers or mentors in the district work as consultants and work one-on-one with individual new teachers as needed.

Mentors also need to meet regularly with other mentors to share ideas and new ways to discuss topics with the new teachers. Mentor collegiality promotes professionalism and brings the role of the mentor/facilitator to a public arena. Professional development and renewal with mentors who work with district coordinators and principals can have a positive impact on the school culture. What will the topics be for any mentor meetings? How could this guide book serve as the curriculum for these meetings?

Evaluation

The evaluation will tell you how successful you have been and what needs to be modified or expanded for the next year. It should be designed as part of the original plan or vision for the induction program before any of the activities are implemented. There should be a section for each area of induction and an overall assessment of the program.

You may also want to find someone in the district who is not passionately involved and can be an impartial observer and evaluator. Using this person as a researcher to interview new teachers, mentors, and principals may offer your committee a new perspective. Keep in mind the larger research question, "Do our teachers stay?"

All these components are important to induction and the initial experience new teachers will have in the district. Use the resources you have to articulate what you would like to do. However, this book is about the mentoring conversations. Mentors are influential in impacting the success of the new teachers.

The Role of the Mentor

Districts and schools may have job descriptions for their mentors depending upon union contracts and state mandates for mentoring. Before beginning any mentoring model, you need to find out what you are required to do, what is optional, and what will be assessed. How a mentor "fits" into the overall induction program is important. Is the mentor the whole program? Is there a plan and an evaluation? All of these are questions that need to be answered to define your role.

This guide is designed to enhance the role of the mentor so that the monthly conversations are planned, rich with discussion possibilities, and providing systematic support based on the new teachers' needs. Topics align with the Interstate New Teacher Assessment and Support Consortium (INTASC), and regular features each month remind the mentors to look at student work as well as to discuss ways to communicate with parents.

This guide encourages the mentor to take a leadership role by organizing time for meetings and suggesting topics of interest. It moves from a more informal role that might have been a "Come and see me if you need help!" role to a more formal role that initiates meetings and asks, "When would you like to meet, the first week of each month?" The guide is for the mentor to use collaboratively with the new teachers as a structure for regular discussions and ongoing reflection and goal setting.

What Should a Mentor Strive For?

I believe mentors should also have their own personal goals in addition to the district requirements. As a mentor, think about what you want to gain during this experience? Mentors should strive to share their own love of teaching and learning with the new teachers. How will you share that?

Studies have shown that mentors have a great impact on new teachers. Being a mentor is complex, and if it is your first time, the task can be daunting. Use the following topics as a guide to think about your role. Feel free to add your own ideas.

An Effective Mentor Relates to Content Knowledge

Many mentors support and nurture new teachers and actually never talk about the curriculum they are teaching. They leave that to professional developers or other teachers. Of course, if the mentor assigned is out of the content area, then there is already a disconnect between the mentor and the new teachers. Certainly emotional support is necessary, but lots of new teachers' stress comes from teaching the content area. How can you as a mentor connect to the content knowledge? Three ways to connect with content are:

1. Share your love for the content areas you teach. How do you demonstrate that love? How do the students know you love your content?
2. Share the curriculum materials you have saved, developed, and bought over the years and encourage the new teachers to use them.
3. Introduce the new teachers to professional resources, organizations, and journals in the content areas

An Effective Mentor Is a Good Teacher

If mentors need to go beyond the emotional support level with new teachers, then they need to be able to talk about instructional practice and effective planning. The mentor needs to be comfortable demonstrating and discussing all of the INTASC Principles.

In addition to discussing these principles, the mentor needs to understand them, be able to model them, and assist the new teachers in doing the same. Each month in Part II highlights one or more INTASC Principles so they can be discussed throughout the school year.

INTASC Principles

Interstate New Teachers Assessment and Support Consortium

- **PRINCIPLE 1 Making content meaningful**
  The teacher understands the central concepts, tools of inquiry, and structures of the discipline(s) he or she teaches and creates learning experiences that make these aspects of subject matter meaningful for students.
- **PRINCIPLE 2 Child development and learning theory**
  The teacher understands how children learn and develop and can provide learning opportunities that support their intellectual, social, and personal development.
- **PRINCIPLE 3 Learning styles/diversity**
  The teacher understands how students differ in their approaches to learning and creates instructional opportunities that are adapted to diverse learners.
- **PRINCIPLE 4 Instructional strategies/problem solving**
  The teacher understands and uses a variety of instructional strategies to encourage students' development of critical thinking, problem solving, and performance skills.
- **PRINCIPLE 5 Motivation and behavior**
  The teacher uses an understanding individual and group motivation and behavior to create a learning environment that encourages positive social interaction, active engagements in learning, and self-motivation.
- **PRINCIPLE 6 Communication/knowledge**
  The teacher uses knowledge of effective verbal, nonverbal, and media communication techniques to foster active inquiry, collaboration, and supportive interaction in the classroom.
- **PRINCIPLE 7 Planning for instruction**
  The teacher plans instruction based upon knowledge of subject matter, students, the community, and curriculum goals.
- **PRINCIPLE 8 Assessment**
  The teacher understands and uses formal and informal assessment strategies to evaluate and ensure the continuous intellectual, social, and physical development of the learner.
- **PRINCIPLE 9 Professional growth/reflection**
  The teacher is a reflective practitioner who continually evaluates the effects of his or her choices and actions on others (students, parents, and other professionals in the learning community) and who actively seeks out opportunities to grow professionally.
- **PRINCIPLE 10 Interpersonal relationships**
  The teacher fosters relationships with school colleagues, parents, and agencies in the larger community to support students' learning and well-being.

Source: http://cte.jhu.edu/pds/resources/intasc-principles.htm

An Effective Mentor Promotes Equity and Social Justice

Teaching is complicated. Students in today's classrooms are diverse and growing increasingly more diverse. New teachers bring assumptions, biases, and stereotypes into the classroom that may not serve the student population or the society in which these students live. How will you as a mentor discuss these complicated issues? How will you mentor for equity and social justice? What will that look like?

Your classroom teaching and procedure will illustrate the approaches to teaching all students equitably. How you teach students whose first language is not English and how you provide opportunities for all students is valuable information for a beginning teacher who has no experience doing this.

An Effective Mentor Makes Student Learning a Priority

In this age of standardized tests, outcomes, and value-added teaching, new teachers need to know how and when to focus of assessment. Whatever the measure, the goal is student learning. Are students learning and how do you know? Working with new teachers every month to look at student work together will keep student learning in the forefront of the discussions.

An Effective Mentor Is a Confidential Colleague

New teachers are not student teachers. They do not need to be supervised. They will have the principal or department chair doing that. They need honest, clear colleagues who are willing to trust them and be trusted by them. They need someone who will not repeat what they see going on in their classroom if it is not going well. Seven ways to be a colleague could be:

1. Maintaining a positive outlook no matter what. Demonstrating enthusiasm, encouragement, patience, kindness, and attention to high standards for teaching and confidence in their success.
2. Accepting the new teachers wherever they are in their development. If they are alternate route teachers, their initial experience may require different approaches or more time on certain topics in this guide.
3. Developing a trusting relationship that allows the new teachers to share their ideas and expertise with you.
4. Making time to meet with the new teachers regularly. Using the *Plan* ideas in this guide to give you a structure for these meetings and the *Act*ivities to provide possible topics for rich discussions.
5. Providing honest, ongoing feedback to new teachers when asked and only when asked.
6. Listening to new teachers ideas, problems, needs, and responding to them in helpful ways.
7. *Reflect*ing and *Set*ting *Goals* at the end of each month to acknowledge what has been done and where you need to go next.

You may have your own "effective mentor" ideas based on your personal experiences being mentored or past experiences as a mentor. Add them to this list and acknowledge what you would like to strive for in your role as an effective mentor of new teachers.

Expanding the One-to-One Model of Mentoring

One-on-one mentoring is expensive, and some districts just can't afford it. Release time, substitutes, mentor training, matching, and providing resources for each new teacher separately may not be the only way to provide induction support. As previously discussed, it makes sense to work in small mentor/facilitated groups. It not only is cost effective, it actually builds a community of new teachers. New teachers actually prefer to be connected to other new teachers, even when they are not exactly at their level or in their content area. They can relate to each other, socialize a bit, and share survival stories. Keeping new teachers isolated with separate mentors may not be in their best interest, nor is it effective in integrating them into the school culture. There may be times when one-on-one mentoring is needed and wanted by individual new teachers for specific topics. As a mentor you can differentiate your mentoring and meet these needs.

Differentiated Mentoring

New teachers are like the students in your classrooms. They are all different and require different types of support at different times during the year. Many induction and mentoring programs provide a one-size-fits-all model to their new teachers. All-or-nothing type approaches like this may not be serving the new teachers. Modify your mentoring discussions to include small subgroups that may be interested in certain topics. Let the other new teachers be free to attend or not. Choice is key to induction and mentoring. New teachers usually know what they need and what is stressing them out. As you read through the Part II Month-by-Month Guide, think about how to offer the discussions as electives. Would it be possible for new teachers to choose to attend some? Will some topics be required? How will you decide? Think about how you will differentiate your mentoring to meet the needs of your diversely prepared new teachers.

Five Principles for Effective Mentoring

In the workshops I do for mentors and cooperating teachers I have discovered that most of what I have to say relates to one of these five guiding principles. I use them as the basis for the workshops to highlight the roles of the mentor. As you read through them, see how they become real for you.

Acknowledging Who You Are and What You Bring to the Mentoring Experience

Who you are as a person, a teacher, and a colleague impacts the way in which you will mentor any new teachers. What do you bring to the mentoring relationship? What have your experiences been as a mentor or being mentored? Have they been positive or negative? Take some time to think about your strengths and your biases. Use the August Activities pages to record your information and use it to acknowledge what you are bringing to the relationship and the role. What would you like to change?

Don't forget to think about who the new teachers are and who they are not. They are new to the profession, the district, and the school. They are not experienced teachers. They may be young, just graduated from college, or they may be older career changers. Both groups have needs that may be very different. New young teachers have shared with me that they don't like mentors referring to them as their sons or daughters because it makes them feel they are not colleagues. Career changers may look like they have a handle on life because they worked in business or have raised a family. They sometimes feel uncertain about classroom management and behavior issues, yet get the impression their mentors think they should know how to do this because they are older. The may be older, but they are still new to the profession and at that initial stage.

New teachers have shared that they want praise and encouragement, but they want it to be specific. Sometimes they don't even know what they are doing that makes a lesson go smoothly. New teachers want those connections to the important people in the building that you know. They also want to be able to show off and share some things with you and other teachers in the school. Acknowledge what you bring to mentoring and what the new teachers bring.

Building Relationships with New Teachers

All the books talk about trust and relationships. Of course you know this is important, but how do you actually begin? One way to begin the process is to create a relationship profile with each one of your new teachers. Find out how you are alike or different by completing the questions in the table. Use the information to discuss different perspectives and how these differences add to teaching and learning. Your goal in mentoring should not be to create a clone of you, but rather to assist a new teacher in uncovering his or her own strengths and teaching styles.

Creating Opportunities for Quality Conversations

This guide is all about creating opportunities for quality conversations. In fact, it goes beyond conversation to discussions that are formal and rich in the opportunities they bring to both the mentor and the new teacher. Mentoring does not mean talking. Many mentors feel a responsibility to tell and share everything they have learned in the past years to help the new teachers. They do this with compassion and empathy—and sometimes without thinking that this might not be the best way for the new teacher to embrace the initial year of teaching. So how can "quality discussions" make a difference?

Discussion and communication imply that talking and listening are going on. Because mentors have all the information that they believe the new teachers need, they tend to talk and tell. Has this happened to you? Some mentors will say, "I ask the new teachers what they need and they say they don't know, so I tell them." This may be the case in several meetings for you as well. The key is to balance the talking and the listening so the new teachers have an entry point into the conversation or discussion. Sometimes writing works for new teachers. Using the Reflections at the end of each chapter may bring out the new teachers' needs in ways they would not state. Mentors are powerful, important people to new teachers. You may not feel that way, but you hold the keys to the kingdom. Be conscious and aware of the opportunities you provide for new teachers to talk.

Do You Really Listen?

How many times have we been able to do three things at the same time? Correcting papers while walking around the room and giving a student "the look" to stop talking? If a new teacher walked in and asked a question at that time, it would be unlikely that he or she would get anyone's full attention. It just isn't the right time for a conversation. Perhaps you could give a quick response to a question, but you know this is not the time for a quality discussion.

The Relationship Profile

For the Mentor and New Teacher

Directions: Through informal conversations, Activities, planned discussions, or an interview complete the table to find out where you and the new teachers are alike and different. Feel free to add your own columns to the table. What would you like to know about each other? Complete one for you and each new teacher with whom you are working.

Topics	**Philosophy of Teaching** ***What do we believe?*** ***Why did we choose teaching?*** ***Will we teach for a career?***	**Career Stage and Age** ***How do we compare?*** ***What are our life issues?*** ***What is happening in or lives right now?*** ***How does it impact teaching and mentoring?***	**Teaching and Learning Styles** ***How do we teach and how do we like to learn?*** ***How do we like feedback?***	**Personality and Life Goals** ***How do we interact with others and what are our priorities in life?***
New Teacher		First year! Age: Could be 22 or 52!		
Mentor		How many years old? How many years as a mentor? How many years as a teacher? How many schools?		
Similarities and Differences—What Shows Up				

Acknowledging diverse perspectives and respecting these differences publicly promotes a trusting relationship. This is one way to build a relationship with the new teachers. Confidentiality is critical to trust. How will you keep these new teachers' perspectives confidential?

Know the difference between a short conversation about something specific and an in-depth discussion related to student learning or a topic of choice. This guide encourages you to make time for these discussions, where you can really listen and make eye contact with the new teachers. Ask yourself, "Am I really listening, or am I thinking about what I want to say next?" Mentors need to be active listeners who don't judge, preach, or lecture to the new teachers. What are some barriers to actively listening?

- If you assume you know what the speaker is going to say, you probably are not actively listening.
- If you are easily distracted and can't maintain eye contact, you probably are not actively listening.
- If you want to argue with the new teachers about their perspectives, you probably are not actively listening.
- If you want total control of the conversation during a meeting, you probably are not actively listening.
- If you draw a conclusion before the speaker is finished, you probably are not actively listening.
- If you are daydreaming or writing your shopping list, you probably are not actively listening.
- If you are tired, you probably are not actively listening.

What other barriers can you think of? How will you overcome the barriers to listening?

Mentoring Styles

You will certainly bring you own mentoring style to this experience. How you teach may relate to how you mentor. Ask yourself the following questions:

- Do I like to talk and explain concepts verbally? Then you probably will like to set up discussions that you can facilitate with the new teachers. Using the Activities will probably be most useful.
- Do I like to write and see concepts on paper? Then you probably will find the Reflections very useful.
- Do I enjoy visual displays and drawing? Then you probably will want to apply the Activities to a bigger picture for the new teachers.
- Do I enjoy touching and moving? Then you will probably want to demonstrate lessons for the new teachers and share the materials you have in your classroom.

As a mentor you will need to create the opportunities for quality discussions by making the time for them to occur. Using the Planning guide and the calendar can help, but only you as the mentor can make the commitment to this time.

Participating in Ongoing Reflection

An area that often gets dropped from very busy schedules is reflection. Who has time? It sounds like a good idea, but it just never seems to fit. This guide includes one form of reflection that is quick and easy for the new teachers and for you. The reflection bubbles have one short prompt in each of them designed to elicit a response. The responses can later be discussed or just saved as reminders of what you both were thinking at the time at the end of that month.

Other ways to reflect are certainly encouraged if you have time or if you enjoy writing. A journal is one effective way to keep track of your mentoring experience, including your mentoring thoughts, challenges, and ideas. Many teachers do maintain a journal. Another way to reflect is a dialogue journal. This allows the new teacher and the mentor to communicate and reflect while writing back and forth. Hard copy journals can be kept in a mutually convenient place. One person starts the conversation and the other writes back. This is a quick and easy way to answer questions during the school day if the mentor is in the same building. No one has to be interrupted, and the answer to the question would be there at the end of the day. Of course, email provides an easy alternative to the dialogue journal. The chats could go beyond the one-on-one and all new teachers could participate in reflecting on a topic.

Reflection can also be part of an ongoing inquiry into practice that may be part of your school community. Are the teachers encouraged to complete action research in your schools? Do the new teachers know how to do research and write inquiry questions? Reflecting on practice is crucial to moving ahead with the new teachers. How will you incorporate it into your mentoring and induction program?

Maintaining a Professional Community of Learners

This guide is really about creating a professional community with the new teachers. If there is only one new teacher entering the school, then your role may be to integrate this teacher into the existing community of learners. How will you do this? Do you agree that this is valuable to do? How will you assist the new teacher in navigating the school culture so he or she can be part of the school? If there are several or many new teachers, how will you promote collegiality with the more experienced teachers? Some experienced teachers, who may not be mentors, are not as welcoming to new teachers, especially if new teachers are given special privileges and have reduced duties. How does this impact the professional community at your school?

Teaching is also part of a wider community that includes professional organizations and teacher unions. Including new teachers in all of these activities is not only important, it is vital to the life of the organizations. New teachers have shared that they have been introduced to the teachers' union by getting a bill that said they had to join. How will you introduce the new teachers to the union? What is the union doing to mentor and support its new members? There are often professional activities for new members and leadership opportunities within the union that may interest the new teachers. Presentations at union conferences and sharing sessions provide audiences for new teachers.

Professional organizations also offer journals, conferences, and materials that can enhance the new teachers' experiences the first year. Some new teachers are just not ready. You will have to decide how and when to introduce the new teachers in your district to these valuable resources.

Don't forget to create your own professional community of mentors. Mentors need support too. Setting up meetings and new opportunities for professional development can refresh and reinvigorate you. Renewal is often cited as a side benefit for the mentor. Give yourself time to acknowledge your renewal.

Mentoring *In Action?* What Does That Mean?

This guide is titled *Mentoring In Action* because as a mentor you will be "in action" when you are doing this work. You most likely will be teaching full time or on a reduced teaching load if you have the resources in your district to do that. The mentoring is being done while the new teachers are on the job. Mentoring cannot be done prior to the teacher's first year. It is not something that can be taught ahead of time or learned and memorized. It is a "learn as you go" model. This collaborative guide offers a road map for the mentoring discussion journey that can assist you in knowing what to talk about, but it doesn't have all the answers. You already know that there will be detours along the way. That's the nature of the work. Staying with the process, being "in action" with the new teachers means you will be responding to their needs as they engage in the initial year of teaching. Enjoy the ride.

Month-by-Month Mentoring

A Guide to Quality Discussions between Mentors and New Teachers

Why Do We Need a Mentoring Curriculum?

Many induction programs that have a mentoring component simply assign you to a new teacher as a mentor at the beginning of the year and say "go mentor." They know you are a good teacher and that you want to help new teachers. They give you a log and say record the hours you meet with your new teachers and pass it in at the end of the year for your stipend (if you are lucky). What you also know is that you might need a little more direction than that. Even if you feel confident and competent as a teacher, you might not feel the same as a mentor. So what do you do? You read about mentoring, you talk with other mentors, and you talk to the new teacher and tell him or her to come to ask you anything at any time. Then you wait for the new teacher to come to you. Some of you may even design your own curriculum and be proactive, but most of you will wait until the new teacher has a question or a crisis.

This collaborative guide is based on the concept that mentors are teachers who can guide new teachers through the school year in a more organized and structured way. This curriculum doesn't rely on the new teachers' being in the driver's seat (since they don't know how to drive yet), it puts the mentor in control of the agenda. This doesn't mean the new teachers don't have input. It means they don't have to initiate the conversations.

As with your students, some really like to know the schedule and the routine. That is why you write it on the board. This curriculum does that for new teachers. It lays out the year for them in a structured way. Mentors often start off strong in August or September and tire after the New Year. This guide is designed to keep mentors and new teachers talking through the entire school year. It is designed to reduce anxiety for new teachers, because they know they will see their mentors several times a month at regularly planned meetings.

Your district may be able to provide in-service credit for the new teachers and for you, for that matter. In-service credit allows you to move across the salary schedule and earn extra money. Find out how you could document the meetings for your district and give everyone credit for participating. State induction programs often require districts "do something." Why not make it valuable for all participants and you as well?

A Month-by-Month Timeline for Mentoring

This section of the book is organized by months because that is how a school year operates. If you are working in a year-round district, or if you begin in August, modify these months to meet your needs. The month is not as important as the developmental approach to the mentoring curriculum. As mentors, we want to give the new teachers everything at once at the orientation. What new teachers tell us is that it is too much too soon. This guide is organized to break it up into smaller bite-sized pieces. No one can eat a whole meal in one bite!

You may find that you want to skip around and discuss December Activities in October—that doesn't matter at all. What matters is that each month you are discussing the issues relevant to your new teachers. Modify, skip around, add, delete, do what works for you. The key is that every INTASC Principle will get discussed if you follow this curriculum, and all key topics will be addressed at some point during the school year. You can be sure of that because you will be initiating the discussion, not waiting for the new teacher to bring it up. Let's face it, even with the best of intentions, we all forget to review certain things with our new teachers if they are not written down. With a curriculum, we are guaranteed to touch on the important topics.

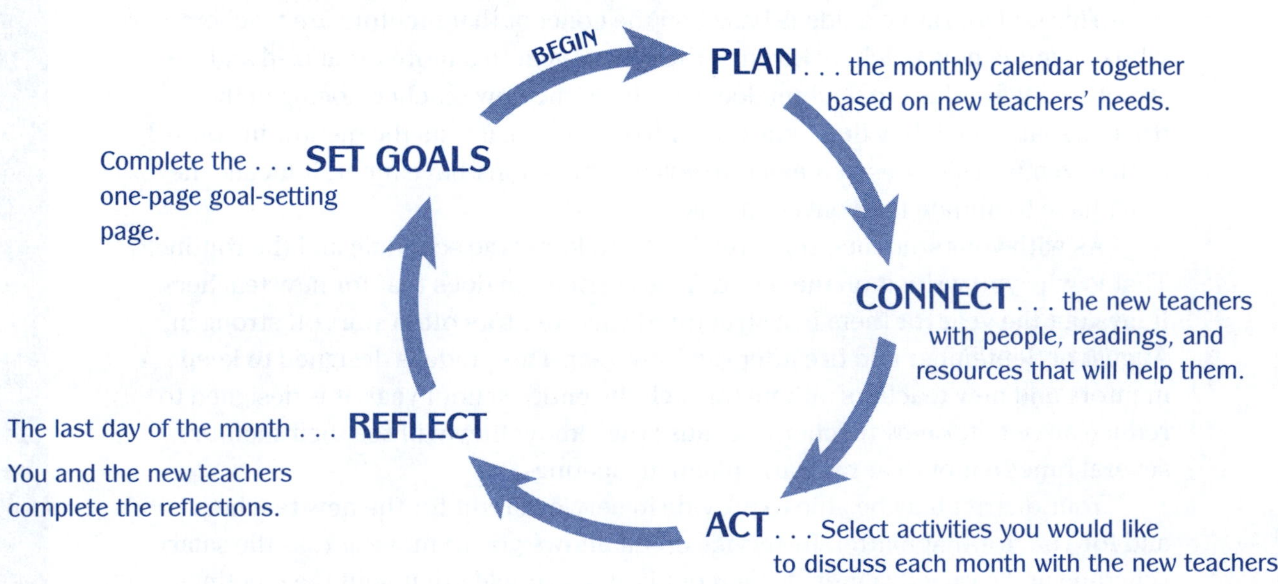
A Month-by-Month Timeline for Mentoring
The Process for an Effective New Teacher Support Mentor
BEGIN
PLAN . . . the monthly calendar together based on new teachers' needs.
CONNECT . . . the new teachers with people, readings, and resources that will help them.
ACT . . . Select activities you would like to discuss each month with the new teachers.
The last day of the month . . . REFLECT
You and the new teachers complete the reflections.
Complete the . . . SET GOALS
one-page goal-setting page.

Another important concept is that even though the topics are divided up, certain ones need to be repeated each month, such as communicating with parents. Actually, everything in this guide happens every month, it is just that you can't discuss all the topics at once. Teaching is complex work that needs to be teased apart to analyze and discuss.

Each chapter contains repeating pages that are in the same order each month. The month always begins with a cover page that includes the following features to focus your attention and provide a context for the discussions.

The Cover Page

What is on it?	Why is it there?
Quote from a student in grade 1–12	This work is all about student learning. The quotes remind us of them and provide a context for the month.
Title of the chapter	This topic gives the discussions a purpose and a focus for the month. Chapter titles all relate to the timing in the year or an INTASC Principle.
New Teacher Phase and typical quote from a new teacher at this time of year	Each month brings the new teachers to new phases. These are reminders of where your new teachers might find themselves during the year.
INTASC Principles	INTASC Principles that relate to the title of the month are included to integrate standards into the discussion.

The cover is followed by a one-page narrative and "What do we want to talk about when we meet this month?" Sample questions that new teachers may ask you and sample questions you could ask them provide you with a preview of what you could discuss this month. Listening to their questions and learning what their needs are will assist you in differentiating the mentoring you will provide.

The mantra for the guide is PLAN, CONNECT, ACT, REFLECT, and SET GOALS. These are concrete, consistent, practical terms that will engage you and the new teachers in your meetings and quality discussions. They can become natural and systematic. You will know the mantra works when the new teachers say, "We can't go to the next month yet, we haven't reflected or set goals yet." Each verb adds an "action" for Mentoring in Action and provides an array of options to choose from. You don't need to do them all—just one will integrate the term with the new teachers and keep them Planning, Connecting, Completing Activities, Reflecting, and Setting Goals. This is an important routine and skillset for any teacher lesson plan. The new teachers can apply it to their own classrooms too.

Use these pages like you would a journal. Write in them, scribble, doodle, make notes, and save them for future reference.

PLAN

Two pages: One allows you to find out what the new teachers need and what you want to share. The other is a planning calendar to schedule and record your meeting times. One "first week of the month" hour-long meeting is suggested to kick off the month. Other meetings may be held before, during, or after school for shorter times. Some contact should be made each week.

CONNECT

One page: In response to what the new teachers need, use your networks of people, readings, and technology to connect them to existing resources. Let them find websites for you and share them at a meeting.

ACT

Multiple pages: One-page "first week of the month" meeting and multiple Activities pages for each month. The agenda for the first week guides you through the process. This is where you and the new teachers get to select the pages that are most meaningful and useful for your discussions. Some pages may be copied and just given to new teachers for reference. Each chapter will have several choices that pertain to the INTASC Principles and the chapter topic.

In addition to the topic choices that will vary each month, there will be repeating Activities each month for the following topics:

Classroom and Behavior Management Issues
Looking at Student Work
Communicating with Parents
Observing New Teachers (January–June)
Preparing a Professional Portfolio (January–June)

REFLECT

Two pages: The last day of the month on your own compete the Reflection and the Set Goals sheets. Make a copy of the Reflection for the new teachers and ask them to bring them to the "first week of the next month meeting." Each reflection also allows the new teachers to add their own thoughts in addition to responding to the prompts.

SET GOALS

One page: This is an opportunity to take a final look at the month and record your impressions of the new teachers' needs and where you would like to begin the next month.

The guide begins in August with two orientation agendas because you may want to be part of the component of the district induction program. If your district does not offer orientations, you may want to include them as part of your mentoring experience.

Mentoring in Action

Month-by-Month Mentoring

August

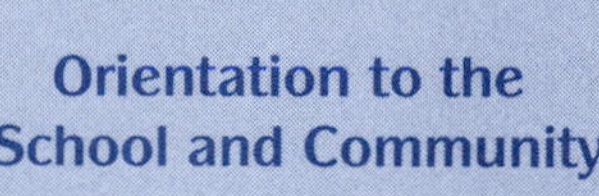

Orientation to the School and Community

Space, Procedures, Resources, Values, and Culture

September

Brginning the School Year Successfully

Creating a Community of Learners in the Classroom

October

Teaching for Understanding

Planning and Delivering Effective Instruction

November

Assessing Diverse Learners

How Do Teachers Know Students Have Learned?

December

Maintaining Balance

Teaching and Keeping the Students Interested

January

Beginning a New Calendar Year

Looking Back and Moving Forward

February

Engaging Students in the Curriculum

Focus on Content through Active Inquiry

March

Collaborating with New Teachers

Observing and Building a Trusting Relationship

April

Standards

Creating Meaningful Standards-Based Learning Experiences for Students

May

Assessing Students' Progress

High-Stakes Tests and Teacher Assessment

June

Completing the Year

Paperwork, Relationships, and Closing a Room

August

Good teachers care about their students, know who they are, and would go to any length to help them get the education they deserve. —High School Student

Orientation to the School and Community

Space, Procedures, Resources, Values, and Culture

New Teacher Phase: Anticipation

"I'm so excited to have my own classroom!"

INTASC Principles

Introduce the new teacher to INTASC Principles 1–10. A complete list is available on page 7 in Part I. Each month one or two principles will be reviewed in more depth to ensure all principles are discussed in the first year. District evaluation standards should also be reviewed throughout the school year and compared to INTASC Principles.

Orientation to the School and Community

Space, Procedures, Resources, Values, and Culture

Mentoring a new teacher is exciting and exhausting work. As a mentor, you have an opportunity to impact that first year by providing support, successful ideas, resources, and an insight to the culture of your school and its surrounding community. Many of us did not have mentors when we began our work in schools, and we know how painful it was to be isolated and alone in the classroom. This guide will ensure you have a road map for your discussions.

This *Month-by-Month Mentoring Guide* can be used with one new teacher or with a small group of new teachers. If you have more than one new teacher, even if they are at different grade levels, it is important to bring them together so they can learn from each other. Most new teachers appreciate group mentoring meetings, because they gain new ideas and find out they are not alone. August is an opportunity for you to orient your new teachers to the school and the community. It is really important for any new teachers to understand the context in which they are doing their teaching. Who are the students? What are their cultures? What does the school value? What is the mission statement for the school, and do teachers, students, parents, and administrators honor it?

Create a "survival" guide for your new teachers (see the Activities pages this month) and share it with them. There is a lot more to teaching than preparing lessons. Even though the new teachers are excited to be in their first classrooms, they will not understand or know your school procedures. Be patient, be resourceful, and assist them in getting organized. Beginning in August before the students arrive is a plus to any mentoring program, so use this time to your advantage.

Use the pages this month to . . . Plan your monthly meetings by deciding what you would like to talk about as well as to set meeting dates for the month, think about how you will *Connect* your new teachers to available resources, select *Act*ivities that make sense for you to discuss, *Reflect* at the end of the month, and *Set Goals* for next month. Use all of these process pages as a guide to enrich the quality of your monthly mentoring conversations.

What Do We Want to Talk about When We Meet This Month?

Invite you new teachers to write down a short list of questions and bring them to your first meeting. Sometimes new teachers don't know what to ask their mentors because they have never done this before, so you may use the questions below as a guide for your discussions throughout the month.

New Teachers' Possible Questions:

1. Who are my students and their families?
2. What do I need to know about the community?
3. What do I need to know about this school and its procedures for opening a school year and a new classroom?
4. What values, expectations, or cultural norms are in operation in this school and the community?
5. Is there a written mission statement for the school?
6. Do you have any suggestions for me as I set up my first classroom?
7. How do I get materials for my classroom and my students?
8. Are there any restrictions or expectations for setting up my classroom space?

List the other questions your new teachers brought to the meeting so you will have them for your next mentoring cycle.

As a Mentor, You Can Ask Questions, Too!

Try to ask more questions to learn about your new teachers, rather than telling them how things should be done.

Mentor's Possible Questions:

1. What do you already know about this community?
2. What are you planning to do to prepare your room and why are you doing that?
3. Do you have any experience setting up a classroom?
4. What can I do to assist you right now that would reduce your anxiety?

● PLAN *Agendas and Schedule Meetings*

Plan your monthly meetings, decide when and how you want to Connect with each other as well as others in the school and community, select the Activities from this chapter that make sense for you to discuss, Reflect separately at the end of the end of the month and share your reflection, and Set Goals for next month.

PLAN *Agendas for Monthly Meetings Based on New Teacher Needs*

Planning quality conversations means that the needs of the new teachers must be met. Take time to complete the chart before making decisions about what you will discuss at your monthly mentoring sessions. What makes most sense for you as a mentor to share in August to assist the new teachers with their needs right now?

Complete this together and save for future discussion. Make a copy for each new teacher if needed.

What is needed and wanted in August?

New Teacher *I need . . .*	Mentor *I want to share . . .*

When Will We Meet?

Plan to meet at times that allow you to have quality time together without interruptions. Knowing when you will meet reduces anxiety for both of you all month. New teachers look forward to planned meetings.

When will you meet?

How many times during the month?

How long will you meet for quality conversations? Ten, twenty, or thirty minutes? Indicate that on this calendar.

Will your new teacher observe you teach and demonstrate a skill this month?

Will you observe the new teachers this month? Purpose of the observation is . . .

Are there other teachers or community members your new teachers need to connect with this month? Indicate on this schedule.

Make a copy of this calendar for the new teachers. Also put these times into your teaching plan book.

August Calendar

MONDAY	TUESDAY	WEDNESDAY	THURSDAY	FRIDAY

Key: B = before school D = during the day (preparation time or lunch time) A = After school

CONNECT *with People, Readings, Professional Associations, Resources, and Technology*

What resources exist in your school and community that could assist new teachers in setting up their first classrooms?

Directions:

1. Review the answers you both completed in the "What is needed and wanted?" boxes on page 26. What does the new teacher need? What do you want to share? Keep the answers to these questions in mind when you explore possible resources.
2. Copy this Connect page so you both can investigate resources separately. Bring your completed August Plan "What is needed and wanted?" and Connect pages to the next meeting and compare what you both discovered. If you are working with a group of new teachers, make copies of all of their completed Connect pages and distribute the resource ideas to everyone in the group.

CONNECT *with People . . .*

Who in the school building (experienced teachers, other beginning teachers, custodians, secretaries, etc.) may be able to help with August needs?

Who or what agency in the community could provide resources or support for no or low cost?

How can parents be helpful in setting up a classroom, and what are the protocols for inviting them in?

CONNECT *with Readings, Professional Associations, and Resources . . .*

What have you read or used that would assist in setting up a first classroom? New teachers may refer to student teaching courses and readings. Mentors may have professional development resources and books for opening a school year.

CONNECT *with Technology . . .*

Find websites and links that will provide information about:

- The district and community
- The school
- Student and parents
- How to set up a first classroom (search by elementary or secondary)
- First day and week activities (search by elementary or secondary)

● ACTIVITIES: *Select Topics for Quality Discussions*

What Will We Discuss at Our August Orientation Meetings?

This is the beginning of your mentoring experience, and you may only meet with your new teachers once or twice before school begins. Many districts have day-long meetings. Use the agendas and activities below as a guide for your meetings.

✓	*Select the activities that are most meaningful for you and your new teachers*
	PLAN: Orientation Agenda Part 1 (or Day 1)
	ACT 1 What Do You Bring to the Mentoring Experience?
	ACT 2 Before You Meet Your New Teachers
	ACT 3 Getting to Know Your New Teachers' Expectations
	ACT 4 What Do New Teachers Bring to Teaching?
	ACT 5 Orientation to the School and District: Meeting Important People
	ACT 6 Orientation to the Students and Their Families in the Community
	ACT 7 Goals and Expectations for the Mentoring Experience
	ACT 8 Creating a Survival Packet—What New Teachers Need to Know Now
	ACT 9 How New Teachers Can Get the Most out of Being Mentored
	ACT 10 Other Support Systems for New Teachers: University Connections
	ACT 11 The First Days and Weeks
	ACT 12 District Evaluation and Support Sessions for Teacher Induction
	REFLECT and SET GOALS for September: Orientation Agenda Part 2 (or Day 2)

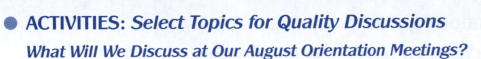

Orientation Agenda Part 1 Day 1*

Meeting Your New Teachers for the First Time

1. Welcome and introductions: Who you are—share your experience as a teacher and a mentor. Use ACTs 1 and 2 to guide you.
2. New teachers' sharing. Use ACT 4 to guide the discussion.
3. Orientation to the school: Review the Important People checklist and other specifics about the school, including teacher unions and parent organizations, dress codes, school mission, and teacher duties. Use ACTs 5 and 8.
4. Overview of the students and their families. Share information about the community and how the new teachers can learn more. Use ACT 6 to guide your planning. Fill it out together at the meeting. You may leave a few answers blank for the new teachers to "find" themselves—do this like a scavenger hunt.
5. Goals and expectations for the mentoring experience. Share yours as a mentor, the district expectations (as well as when they will be assessed by the principal) and allow time for new teachers to share what they expect in the way of support. Use ACTs 3 and 7. Also discuss how new teachers can get the help they need. Use ACTs 10 and 11.
6. Share ideas for the first day and first week of school using ACTs 11 and 12.
7. Close with compliments for each new teacher and small gifts from the school.

*_Note:_ This may be a one-on-one meeting with your assigned new teacher, or it may include small group of new teachers. It will take place typically after the district orientation, or it may be part of the orientation. Have snacks and water or soft drinks available. Hold the meeting in your classroom or another comfortable space where you can meet without interruptions. Modify this sample agenda as needed.

Agenda Part 2 Day 1 or Day 2 *

1. Ask new teachers to complete Reflections in the bubbles and to add two of their own. You need to complete your Reflection as well. This can be done for homework and brought back to another meeting, or it may be your closing activity if you are having an all-day meeting.
2. Share the Reflections with each other and discuss them. You can respond to the areas where they are frustrated or nervous.
3. Complete the Set Goals process together. Be sure your goals match what the new teachers need. Even though they need so much at this time and you are tempted to give them "everything" as a goal, try to focus on the most important things right now. Learning how to prioritize is an important skill for new teachers. What three things are most important for these new teachers?
4. Make copies of the goal sheets for the new teachers. Review the meeting date for September planning meeting. When will you meet, the first week? At that meeting you will decide how to build on these goals and move to the next month's topic.
5. Explain how you will be using the month-by-month mentoring concept as a protocol to ensure that these important topics are discussed in depth during the school year.
6. Close the meeting with compliments for each new teacher and set the next meeting time—the first week of September to complete plans for the month. Exchange phone numbers and emails. Explain how you would like to be contacted before the next meeting if someone needs assistance.

**Note:* Modify this sample agenda as needed.

What Do You Bring to the Mentoring Experience?

1. Think about who your mentors have been. List their names.

   Why were these mentors important to you?

   What were their qualities?

   How will you use your mentors' qualities in this relationship?

2. Think about your experience as a teacher and a mentor. How long have you taught? Have you been a mentor before? What have you learned? How will you apply your mentor learning to this new situation?

3. What is your mentoring philosophy? Complete this sentence.

   I believe ____

4. List three words that capture your beliefs about mentoring new teachers.

   1. ________________ 2. ________________ 3. ________________

5. Briefly describe your role in assisting new teachers in two or three sentences. Be sure to share this with your new teachers.

6. Explain to yourself why you said "yes" to being a mentor.

7. What do you see as your strengths as a teacher? As a mentor?

Before You Meet Your New Teachers

1. Meet with district coordinators to define your roles and responsibilities.
2. Read this text to gain an understanding of the month-by-month mentoring model.
3. Decide where you would like to have your meetings—e.g., the library, a conference room, your classroom. Check with appropriate staff to reserve space if necessary.
4. Create a Survival Kit and invite your colleagues to donate small items, too.

   This could include stickers, school supplies, samples of lessons for the first day or first week, a plant for the classroom, or any other appropriate gift. Present the gift in a welcome to our school presentation. Have each colleague write one small tip that will get the new teachers through that first week of school.
5. Prepare to introduce the new teachers to colleagues at the school. Perhaps host a breakfast or after-school social. Prepare materials that will be useful.
6. What else do you need to do for the district? Log? Paperwork?

Getting to Know Your New Teachers' Expectations

Expectations play a role in new teachers' perceptions about their schools. When the reality of a school does not meet the new teachers' expectations, they get confused and become uncertain about choosing teaching as a profession. The best way to avoid unfulfilled expectations is to invite new teachers to share what they expect at the beginning. Interview each new teacher to discover his or her expectations. Clarify the realities of your school that may not match what new teachers expect.

Ask the new teachers:

1. What behaviors do you *expect from other teachers* at your school? And what do you think they will *expect from you*?

    Some new teachers have responded this way: I expect support, a willingness to share ideas with me, to be included socially, and to have some freedom to teach the way I have been taught. I think teachers will expect me to bring in new methods and new knowledge of technology and to be professional.

    How do your new teachers' responses compare?

    How do these expectations match the reality of your school culture?

2. What behaviors do you expect from other beginning teachers at the school? What do you think they expect from you?

    Some new teachers have responded this way: I expect other new teachers to share their ideas and challenges, to be a shoulder to cry on, to share materials. I think other new teachers will expect the same from me.

    How do your new teachers' responses compare?

    How do these expectations match the reality of your school culture?

3. What behaviors do you expect from school administrators? What do you think they expect from you?

    Some new teachers have responded this way: I expect support, information about the school, a reasonable class, professional guidance, time to talk, positive reinforcement, and feedback.

    How do your new teachers' responses compare?

    How do these expectations match the reality of your school culture?

4. What behaviors do your new teachers expect from you as their mentor?

What Do New Teachers Bring to Teaching?

Most mentors would say that new teachers bring energy, passion, and new ideas into the classroom and the school. If they are supported during their first year, they can actually enhance school culture and spread their enthusiasm to others. Experienced mentors acknowledge the strengths of their new teachers and use them to build community in their grade levels and departments.

New Teacher Profile

I. *Teacher Preparation*

A. Describe your preparation for teaching as defined in your course work. Describe the course that stands out for you as being the best preparation and why. Highlight your content knowledge as well as your methods courses on your transcript.

B. List your previous experiences in schools as a student teacher or previous work with young children or adolescents.

II. *Skills and Experiences*

A. Do you speak a world language? Explain.

B. Do you or have you played or coached sports? Explain.

C. Where have you traveled? Why did you visit these places?

D. Do you have musical, drama, or any arts ability? Explain.

E. What is your level of proficiency with computers and other technology?

F. Other hobbies?

III. *Life Goals*

A. Where do you see yourself in five years? ten years? twenty years?

B. Why did you choose teaching?

IV. *Personal Joys*

A. What gives you joy?

B. What would you like me to know about you?

C.

Bring this completed profile to our first meeting.

Orientation to the School and District: Meeting Important People

Introduce the new teacher to: (provide a written list of names correctly spelled)

- Principals and headmasters as well as assistants that were not part of the interview
- Department chairs that were not part of the interview
- Teachers in the building by grade level and department
- Specialist teachers (art, music, computer, physical education, etc.)
- Bilingual teachers
- Support specialists (guidance, clinical psychologist, nurse, physical therapist)
- Special education teachers (share the model your school is using, i.e., inclusion or pullout)
- Support personnel (secretaries, aides, paraprofessionals)
- Custodians and lunchroom employees
- Parents (volunteer groups or formally organized groups)
- Building-based support teams
- Police officers

School Scavenger Hunt (complete with other new teachers)

Invite the new teachers to find these answers before the next meeting. They can use the website or background information you have provided as well as interview the people listed above.

1. Complete name of the school and why it has this name. How old is the school? Also attach phone, email, website address, and directions to the school with a local map.
2. How many students are enrolled in this school? Diversity of students by ethnicity? Languages spoken? Ages of students by grade level?
3. School hours? When are recesses? Lunches? What are the schedules? Are they blocks?
4. Public transportation available? If so, what is schedule?
5. Theme or mission of the school? How is it portrayed?
6. Organization of school classrooms. Number? Size? Shape of school? Number of teachers per grade level?
7. Profile of the teachers by years of experience. Bilingual?
8. Special programs or activities in this school?
9. What are teachers most proud of in this school?
10. How does this school relate to other schools in the district?

Orientation to the Students and Their Families in the Community

Getting to know the students and the local community is important for any new teacher, especially if the new teacher has moved in from another state.

I. *Interviewing students*

Encourage the new teachers to meet with a few students at the school before the school year begins. These do not have to be students in their classes, but any student who is willing to come into the school to talk with new teachers. Invite the new teachers to create questions. Ask the student presenters to share what they like about this school.

II. *Interviewing Parents*

Encourage the new teachers to meet with parents. Ask the parents to share how they work with teachers in this school. As a mentor, you need to let the new teachers know how parents are used to enhance learning.

III. *Taking a Tour of the Community*

Many school districts provide a tour. If there is not one in the district, encourage the new teachers to take a tour on their own. Highlight the key places the teachers should visit, such as the town hall, the center, neighborhoods, etc.

IV. *Reviewing the Website*

Require all the new teachers to review the website for important information.

Discuss this information at one of your meetings and why it is important to know before the opening of school.

Goals and Expectations for the Mentoring Experience

1. List your own personal goals for this experience:

   a. ____

   b. ____

   c. ____

2. I expect:

   a. ____

   b. ____

   c. ____

3. Verify your expectations with the mentor coordinator to avoid confusion. What does the district expect you to do?

4. What outcomes will you be able to measure as a result of this experience? The new teachers will know and be able to…

5. You will be asking (or have already asked) the new teachers to explain what their expectations are for you as their mentor in ACT 3. Review these expectations and clarify any that you will not be meeting at this time to avoid unfulfilled expectations.

6. How will you know you have been successful as a mentor?

7. How will you be supported during this experience? Will there be a mentor support group for you? Will you all be using month-by-month mentoring as a guide?

Creating a Survival Packet: What New Teachers Need to Know Now!

Collect as many materials listed below as you can and organize them in a binder labeled "Survival Tips."

I. *Materials*
- Schedules (daily, weekly, block, holiday)
- Student and school handbooks with policies
- Mission statements and vision statements
- Curriculum guides for grade levels
- List of faculty with phone numbers
- Class lists
- Report cards and parent communication
- Discipline policies
- Professional development schedule
- State policy for reporting abuse, neglect, or other legal issues

II. *Buzz Words* (here is a sample—add your own)
- Building-based support team
- IEP
- Title I
- Add your local words and explain

III. *Procedures and School Culture Protocols*
- Fire drill and other building exiting procedures
- Protocols and expectations that are not written (how teachers get lunch and where they eat)
- Other school customs for holidays or staff birthdays
- Sending students to the nurse (from colds to crisis—how to know the difference)
- Getting support for students in crisis (home problems that students bring to school)
- Guidelines for referring students for misbehavior (Where do they go? What do you write?)
- Supervisory duties and expectations for new teachers (hall duty, cafeteria, recess duty, bus duty)
- How and where to make copies for lessons
- Location of the books and resources needed to teach
- How to use the library to enhance teaching resources (school or public)

IV. *Building Floor Plan and School Organization*
- Map of school with room numbers and exits clearly labeled (also nurse, office, workrooms, bathrooms, staff lounges)
- Map of schoolyard, where buses drop off, and where students enter and exit
- Policies for setting up classrooms

V. *Teacher Union Information and State Licensing Information*
- Representatives—meeting them with you
- Understanding paying dues
- Reviewing the teacher contract and state requirements

How New Teachers Can Get the Most out of Being Mentored

1. Ask the new teachers to share how they can get the most out of being mentored. List their main ideas here.

2. Based on their ideas and expectations, share your own ideas. Use ACTs 3 and 7 to guide your discussion as well as the three big ideas below.

Mentoring can help you when you . . .

- *Ask questions* (by email, phone, by using a question dialogue journal, or in person).

  A dialogue journal is a book that is set up in the mentor's classroom. If a new teacher has a question, she writes it in the journal. When the mentor has a minute, he responds. The next time the new teacher comes in, she checks it out and perhaps writes another question. This works because it allows the new teacher to write at any time and the mentor to respond when he has a chance. All the questions are also in writing to review at the end of the year. Quick and easy!

- *Visit* your mentor's classroom before or after school on a regular basis.

  Getting to know the systems, routines, and students in another classroom will allow the new teacher to see that some of the issues are the same. All teachers face misbehavior issues and how to handle mounds of paperwork!

- *Make time* to meet with your mentor.

  Time is the essential ingredient for success through reflection. Using this month-by-month mentoring guide will provide the structure for formal discussions, but the new teacher has to see these discussions as important. A ten-minute meeting can really help . . . but the new teacher has to mentally make time for this.

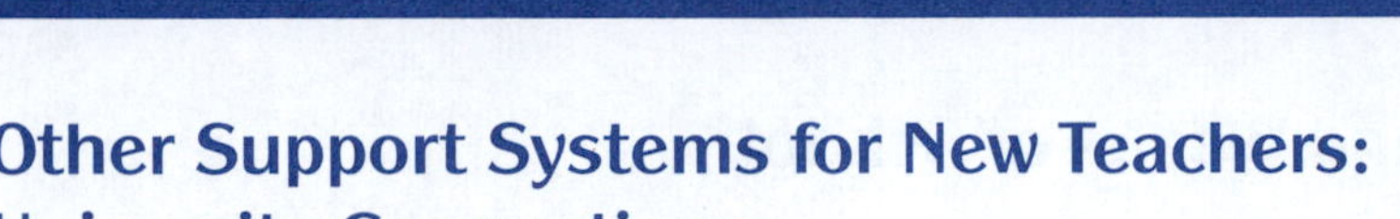

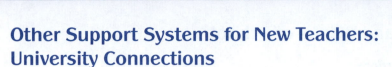

Other Support Systems for New Teachers: University Connections

If your new teachers have been prepared in a teacher preparation program, they may be able to access resources that will assist them in their first years.

Interview the new teachers to find out what is available.

1. Does your university expect to follow its graduates into the first years of teaching? If yes, how is it planning to help? Is it local or online? Do you know professors who could help you?
2. Does your university provide any support for mentor teachers? Online courses or websites? Can I take these courses? Are there any events we should be attending? Professional development workshops that would help us?
3. Is your university partnered with any universities in this area who are providing support to new teachers?
4. What materials do you have from student teaching that you could use right now to get you started?
5. Are you considering a masters degree or other coursework?

For the mentor:

Is there any districtwide program for new teachers and their mentors? How can you use it to support your work?

Review the resources from the New Teacher Center at the University of California, Santa Cruz, by going online. Read mentor guide books and books for the new teachers that you find online and share them at monthly meetings.

The First Days and Weeks of School

Organizing the Classroom

Assist the new teacher in drawing a floor plan for placement of furniture. Ask the new teacher questions as she places furniture. Can all the students see you from that teaching location? Do they need to see you? Draw out possible traffic flow as well as fire exits.

Establishing Routines

Discuss the important routines that need to be established on day 1. How will the new teacher share these routines with the students? Why are they important? Share your routines after the new teacher has shared his ideas. Offer suggestions as needed and allow the new teachers to modify your suggestions.

What to Do the First Day

Share the agendas you have used on the first day of classes. Invite the new teachers to share their ideas for the first day. Learning students' names, perhaps taking a photo of each student, and day 1 orientation activities are important. High school students need to know how to move from one classroom to the next.

Materials for Teaching in the First Weeks

How and where does the new teacher get books, supplies, materials? Assist in this process and help design those beginning of the year lesson plans together. New teachers who can gain confidence in the early weeks with their teaching have a better chance of surviving until the holidays.

What Else Is Important for You to Share?

District Evaluation and Support Sessions for Teacher Induction

Evaluations

When are the new teachers evaluated? How will it be done? By whom—principal or department chair? How many observations will the new teacher have the first year? Get a schedule for the new teachers and discuss the process.

As a mentor, you are not an evaluator. You may, however, assist the new teacher in preparing for the evaluation and provide support along the way if that is appropriate. Information about the evaluation cycle and the expectations for the new teacher as part of the pre- and post-conferences is important. You can play an important role in making sure the new teachers with whom you work have the information they need to participate in the process.

Teacher Induction Support

Many districts provide special professional development sessions on hot topics such as classroom management, special needs modifications, working with English language learners, and other issues. Encourage your new teachers to attend if these are not required. Knowledge is power for a new teacher. Time is always a factor, but this information can only help.

Use this month-by-month mentoring guide as a professional development course if district induction support is not provided. Bring small groups of new teachers together with groups of your colleagues to provide informal sharing. Simply sharing your ideas will provide new teachers with practical, successful ideas and will also make them feel part of a professional group.

Mentoring is only one component of effective teaching induction. Orientation and professional development are also important.

REFLECT *on This Month's Discussions*

Mentor Reflections

Directions: Complete as many of the bubble prompts as you would like after you have finished the activities in the chapter and before you set goals. Add your own prompts to blank bubbles if these prompts do not meet your needs. Ask your new teachers to complete their own reflection bubbles on the next page. Compare and share your reflections at one of your meetings. You may consider using one or two reflection bubbles as topics for future mentoring discussions.

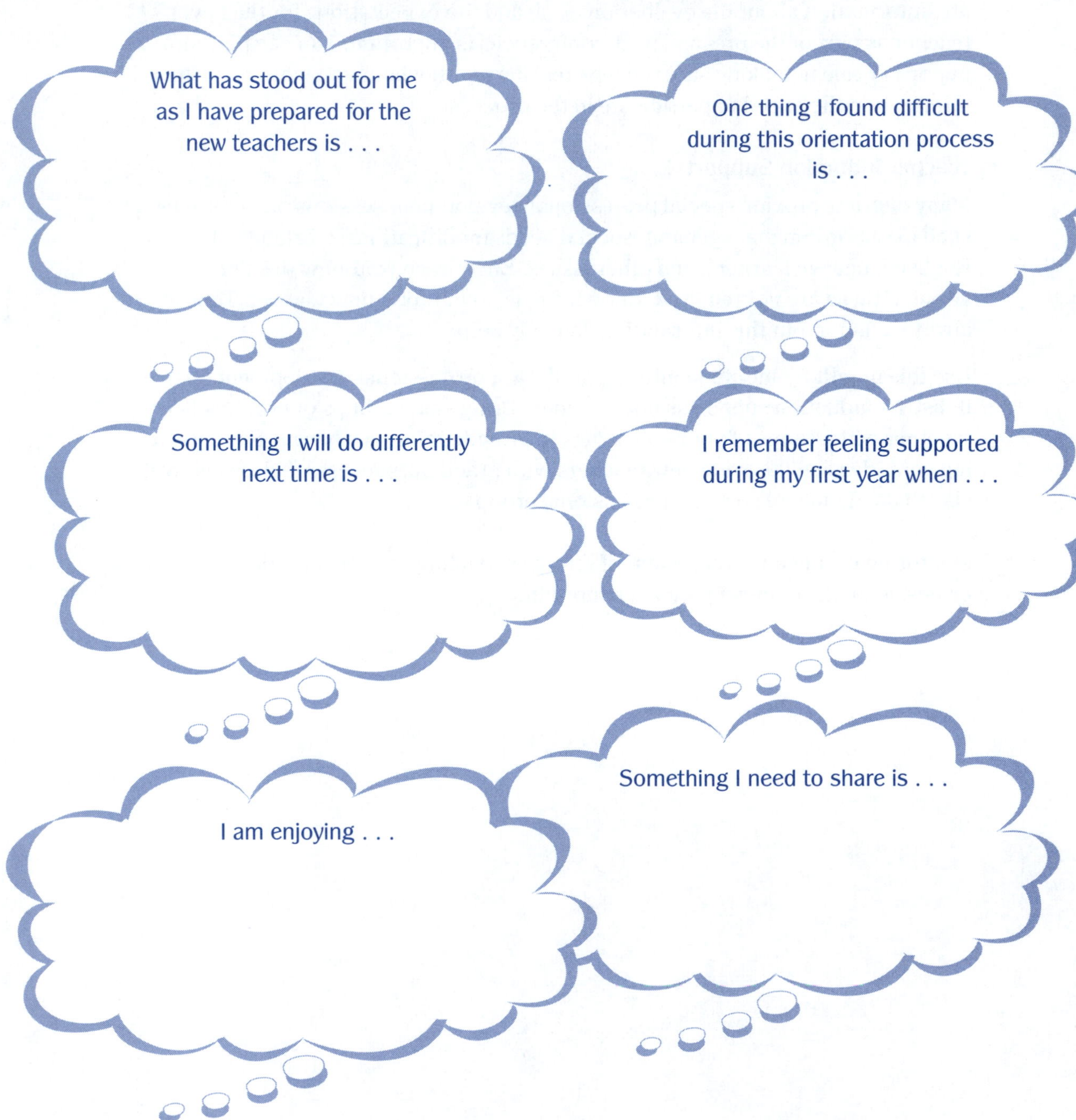

What has stood out for me as I have prepared for the new teachers is . . .
One thing I found difficult during this orientation process is . . .
Something I will do differently next time is . . .
I remember feeling supported during my first year when . . .
I am enjoying . . .
Something I need to share is . . .

New Teacher Reflections

Directions: Complete as many of the bubble prompts as you would like after you have finished the activities in the chapter and before you set goals. Add your own prompts to blank bubbles if the prompts listed do not meet your needs. Compare and share your reflections with your mentor and other new teachers at a scheduled meeting.

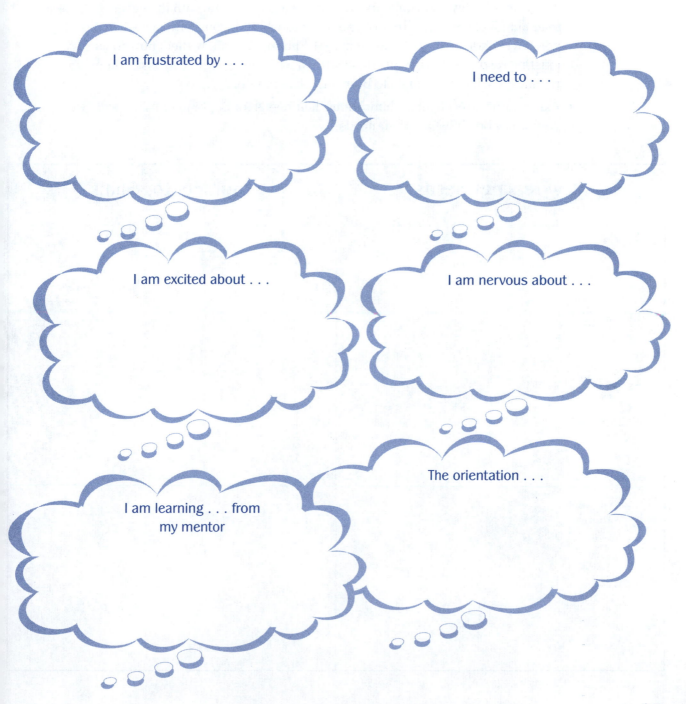

I am frustrated by . . .

I need to . . .

I am excited about . . .

I am nervous about . . .

I am learning . . . from my mentor

The orientation . . .

SET GOALS *for Next Month*

Directions:

- At the end of the orientation formally acknowledge what your new teachers accomplished. Be specific about what was done well.
- Review the PLAN–CONNECT–ACT–REFLECT pages you completed in this chapter to see what you need to revisit next month. Use these for possible goal ideas.
- Ask the new teachers what they need to focus on next month.
- Ask yourself how you would like to share what you know with the new teachers. Will you give a tour of your classroom? Will you share materials you have made? Will you take them to the library and show them how to use existing resources? Will you connect them with people who can assist them regularly? What will you do to be an effective mentor?
- Ask your new teachers to think about their needs for September. What will your goals be? What are their needs?

New Teacher Needs	Your Mentor Goals
1.	1.
2.	2.
3.	3.

September

A good teacher is someone who is helpful, thoughtful, smart, knows how to teach, and loves kids. —Third-Grade Student

Beginning the School Year Successfully

Creating a Community of Learners in the Classroom

New Teacher Phase: Nervous and Ready

"I feel prepared to teach but I don't know what to do the first day."

INTASC Principles

Introduce the new teacher to INTASC Principles 2 and 5.

- **PRINCIPLE 2 Child Development and Learning Theory**
  The teacher understands how children learn and develop and can provide learning opportunities that support their intellectual, social, and personal development.
- **PRINCIPLE 5 Motivation and Behavior**
  The teacher uses an understanding of individual and group motivation and behavior to create a learning environment that encourages positive social interaction, active engagements in learning, and self-motivation.

Beginning the School Year Successfully

Creating a Community of Learners in the Classroom

Setting up a first classroom is exciting and exhausting work. A wise person once said, "Wisdom is not knowing what to do ultimately, it is knowing what to do next." As a mentor, you will work with your new teacher or group of new teachers collaboratively to assist them in understanding what to do next. You, as a mentor, are creating a community of learners between the two of you (or among the group if you are working in mentoring teams), as well as assisting the new teachers in creating a community among their own students in their own classrooms.

Each new teacher will have different needs based on his or her previous experiences and teacher preparation. You will be able to focus on what needs to be done next so you can minimize the anxiety the new teacher will be feeling in September at the opening of school and maximize student learning in each new teacher's classroom this month.

Your new teachers will have questions, emotional ups and downs, and lots of ideas they want to try out this month and this year. You may have to bite your lip so you don't say too much, but rather explore the options with them. Mentoring is not about "telling" but more about "creating" opportunities where your new teachers can discover what to do next. You know they can't learn how to apply all the INTASC Principles in one month, yet you will be tempted to try to give them everything at once. Hold back. Try to focus yourself and become a listener. Mentoring is a lot like good teaching. Students want you to know them and listen to them. There will be time to tell and share the many good ideas you have when appropriate. As a mentor, you will have lots of advice about survival and creating a community of learners. Your challenge will be holding back a bit and allowing the new teacher to experience the process while you guide, question, and assist. This may not be as easy as it sounds, especially in September when there is so much to do.

Working together using this guide as a stepping off point for quality discussions will focus you and allow you to begin the important discussion of creating a community of learners in your classroom. Differentiated mentoring applies here if you are working with more than one new teacher. Assess their needs individually and discuss what is appropriate for each learner.

Use this process as a guide to enrich the quality of your monthly mentoring conversations. Add your own experiences and other mentoring resources as needed. Remember the new teachers bring ideas and expertise, too!

What Do We Want to Talk about When We Meet This Month?

Invite you new teachers to write down a short list of questions and bring them to your first meeting. Sometimes new teachers don't know what to ask their mentors because they have never done this before, so you may use the questions below as a guide for your discussions throughout the month.

New Teachers' Possible Questions:

1. How do I create a community of learners? What does that mean?
2. Can you review how children learn at this age level?
3. How many of my students need support in English language learning and what should I do to help them integrate socially and academically?
4. I need some help setting up routines in my classroom that will avoid misbehavior. Can you share some successful ways for setting up a classroom in September?
5. What are self-motivating strategies for students?
6. What do I do if a student misbehaves?

List the other questions your new teachers brought to the meeting so you will have them for your next mentoring cycle.

As a Mentor, You Can Ask Questions, Too!

Try to ask more questions to learn about your new teachers, rather than telling them how things should be done.

Mentor's Possible Questions:

1. What is your understanding of child/adolescent development?
2. At which level did you complete your student teaching?
3. How confident are you in starting the year?
4. What can I do to assist you right now that will reduce your anxiety?

PLAN *Agendas and Schedule Meetings*

Plan your monthly meetings, decide when and how you want to Connect with each other as well as others in the school and community, select the Activities from this chapter that make sense for you to discuss, Reflect separately at the end of the end of the month and share your reflection, and Set Goals for next month.

PLAN *Agendas for Monthly Meetings Based on New Teacher Needs*

Planning quality conversations means that the needs of the new teacher must be met. Take time to complete the chart before making decisions about what you will discuss at your monthly mentoring sessions. Mentors also have lots to share. What makes most sense for you as a mentor to share in September?

Complete this together and save for future discussion. Make a copy for each new teacher if needed.

What is needed and wanted in September?

New Teacher *I need . . .*	Mentor *I want to share . . .*

When Will We Meet?

Plan to meet at times that allow you to have quality time together without interruptions. Knowing when you will meet reduces anxiety for both of you all month. New teachers look forward to planned meetings.

When will you meet?

How many times during the month?

How long will you meet for quality conversations? Ten, twenty, or thiry minutes? Indicate that on this calendar.

Will your new teacher observe you teach and demonstrate a skill this month?

Will you observe the new teachers this month? Purpose of the observation is . . .

Are there other teachers or community members your new teachers need to connect with this month? Indicate on this schedule.

Make a copy of this calendar for each new teacher. Put these times into your teaching plan book.

September Calendar

MONDAY	TUESDAY	WEDNESDAY	THURSDAY	FRIDAY

Key: B = before school D = during the day (preparation time or lunch time) A = After school

CONNECT *with People, Readings, Professional Associations, Resources, and Technology*

What resources exist in your school and community that could assist new teachers in beginning the school year successfully?

Directions:

1. Review the answers you both completed in the "What is needed and wanted?" boxes on page 50. What does the new teacher need? What do you want to share? Keep the answers to these questions in mind when you explore possible resources.
2. Copy this Connect page so you both can investigate resources separately. Bring your completed September Plan "What is needed and wanted?" and Connect pages to the next meeting and compare what you both discovered. If you are working with a group of new teachers, make copies of all of their completed Connect pages and distribute the resource ideas to everyone in the group.

CONNECT *with People . . .*

Who in the school building (experienced teachers, other beginning teachers, custodians, secretaries, etc.) may be able to help with September needs?

Who or what agency in the community could provide resources or support for no or low cost?

How would parents be included in September "creating a community of learners" activities?

CONNECT *with Readings, Professional Associations, and Resources . . .*

What have you read or used that would assist in creating a community of learners? New teachers may refer to student teaching courses and readings. Mentors may have professional development resources and books that relate to this topic.

CONNECT *with Technology . . .*

Find websites and links that will provide information about:

- Creating learning communities (search by grade level)
- Child development and learning theory (search by grade level)
- Motivation strategies for students (search by grade level)
- Beginning school year activities

● ACTIVITIES: *Select Topics for Quality Discussions*

What Will We Discuss at Our September Meetings?

Each month begins with a formal first week planning meeting where dates and times for discussions are scheduled. Use the agenda in this chapter to guide your meeting. Select Activity pages listed on this page as possible talking points at this meeting or for any other meetings you schedule during the month. Record your meeting dates and time on your Planning calendar. You may decide to assign some Activity pages to the new teacher for completion alone. Use the Appendix for five-, ten-, fifteen-, twenty-, thirty-, and sixty-minute meeting formats you may want to use during the month.

Schedule this meeting during the first week of the month	**PLAN the Monthly Discussions (see sample agenda)**
✓ The Activities you will discuss	**ACT by Selecting Appropriate Topics for Discussions during the Month**
	Activities for September discussions related to *Beginning the School Year* include . . .
	ACT 1 Creating a Community of Learners in Your Classroom
	ACT 2 Getting to Know the Students
	ACT 3 Creating a Classroom Profile
	ACT 4 Learning about Learning Styles
	ACT 5 Establishing Routines
	ACT 6 Rules, Rewards, and Consequences
	ACT 7 First Month of School Issues
	* ACT 8 Classroom and Behavior Management Issues
	* ACT 9 Looking at Student Work
	* ACT 10 Communicating with Parents
	ACT 11 New Teacher Needs
The last day of the month the new teachers and you complete these pages on your own.	**REFLECT and SET GOALS for Next Month** **Give new teachers copies of Reflect and Set Goals pages to bring to the October first week meeting.**

*These three Activities will be offered each month.

• First Week Agenda: Making a Plan for the Month

TOPIC: Beginning the School Year Successfully: Creating a Community of Learners in the Classroom

Have snacks and water or soft drinks available. Hold the meeting in your classroom or another comfortable space where you will be sure you will not be interrupted. Put a colorful sign on your door that says "Mentoring Meeting—Please do not disturb."

First: Welcome and introductions: Invite new teachers to share something that is going well.

Then: Review the August new teacher Reflections.

- How did the new teachers respond? How will this impact what you do next?
- Share any of your Mentor Reflections that are appropriate.

Next: Review the Set Goals page that you completed after the August orientation.

- How will these goals carry over into this month?
- What do we want to talk about when we meet this month?
- Share the possible key questions listed at the beginning of this chapter.
- What most interests the new teachers right now?

Begin: Plan what you will discuss this month use the Planning calendar to set your meeting times. Think about how you should share information with the new teachers. Will you give handouts, a tour of your room, or hold discussions? Review the Activities pages for handouts and discussion ideas. Use the Appendix for five-, ten-, fifteen-, twenty-, thirty-, and sixty-minute meeting templates. Modify Activities and templates as needed.

Network: Complete the Connections page together.

Acknowledge: Recognize what you and the new teachers have done so far instead of focusing on what they don't know. Remind the new teachers that they will complete Reflections and Set Goals pages on their own the last day of the month to bring to the first week meeting the next month.

Share: End the session with compliments for each new teacher and at least one practical idea for beginning the school year. Let new teachers share ideas with each other, too.

Creating a Community of Learners in Your Classroom

1. Discuss the ways you create an environment where all students feel comfortable and respect each other. Share how you include students of other cultures in ways that empower them to be sharing members of the classroom.
2. Invite the new teachers to share what they know about community and team building from their teacher preparation programs.
3. Discuss the following approaches and see if any work for these new teachers.
   - *Integrating student sharing*—Start the day or class with five minutes of student sharing time. Rationale: Students come to school with lots of issues related to their personal lives. Getting to know each other, learning how to listen, and respecting the lives of others can enhance a classroom community.
   - *Creating partnerships in the classroom*—Allow students to work together, sit together, support each other. Rationale: Students want to talk to each other. By organizing it, new teachers can structure the sharing and use it for academic purposes. For example: When a student is absent, his or her partner can collect all the work and share what needs to be made up.
   - *Organizing teams*—Learning teams can make school more engaging for students who want to interact. Teams can work on projects, create team slogans, and challenge each other in academic ways. Rotate teams periodically to include all learners. Rationale: Teamwork is more fun for some students and teaches students how to work together.
   - *Giving compliments*—Students can give each other compliments at the end of the day. Rationale: Everyone likes to hear he or she is doing something well. Model the compliments process with students. Positive words create caring communities.
   - What are your ideas for creating positive learning environments?

Getting to Know the Students

Listening to students, understanding their needs, and responding to their suggestions are important ways to build relationships. Many first-year teachers make the mistake of being a friend to students and then have difficulty being a teacher later in the year. Use the ideas on this page to assist your new teachers in getting to know their students.

Some ways to learn about your students . . .

1. *Create an Interest Survey.* Ask students to complete a short-answer survey. Here are some sample questions:
   - What do you like most about school?
   - What do you think your strengths are in the classroom?
   - How do you learn best?
   - What is your favorite subject? Why?
   - What language do you speak at home?
   - Have you ever traveled to another country?
   - What could I help you learn this year?
   - What do you wish you could do in school?
   - What is your favorite sport or hobby?
   - Do you play a musical instrument?

   Adapt questions to meet the needs of your age group. You may have to read the questions to younger children and write their answers on the board, or they can circle a set of smile faces to show their opinion.

   Short version: Select one or two questions and have students write the answers on the front and back of an index card. Make sure they write their names on the cards!

   Read the answers carefully and note the diverse needs and skills presented in this information. You may want to create a grid with names and skills to chart the whole class. Use this information to create a classroom profile.
2. *Take photographs of each student.* Students love it, and it will help you learn their names and faces. This may be more appropriate for younger students. A whole-class photograph is fun for all age groups.
3. *Interview as many students as possible.* Ask them to talk about their experiences in school and how they feel they learn best. You may want to audiotape these talks for future reference. Be sure to get permission from cooperating teachers, students, and parents.
4. *Interview your mentor teacher.* Ask him to identify students with special needs who will require modifications in their work and any other students who should be noted.
5. *What are your ideas for getting to know your students?*

Creating a Classroom Profile

With your mentor teacher's assistance, create a profile of the students in your classroom. If you are teaching secondary or middle school, select one of your classes to review. Find the information about the students through observing, their class record, a written survey, interviews, a class questionnaire, and talking with other teachers. The more you know about the class, the easier it is to create and maintain a positive learning environment.

List the names of the students and complete the chart by writing one or two descriptive words for each category. When complete, you will have a summary of the class you will be working with this semester. Feel free to replace these categories with those you would find more useful.

STUDENTS	Gender	Culture	Age	Language	Musical Ability	Artistic Ability	Athletic Ability	Learning Style	Learning Need

Learning about Learning Styles

Students learn in many ways. Being able to recognize the differences will assist you in designing lessons and bringing the students together as a team. Diversity of learning styles makes the team more resourceful, yet students also need to be aware of the differences so they don't argue about their different approaches.

Check your own preferred learning styles and compare with your mentor teacher. Review current learning-style theories and translate that theory into practice by observing students. Many of these theorists have short learning-style tests that are available for use. Check with the school guidance counselor or adjustment counselor for details.

Ask the students how they think they learn best. Students know what they prefer and which methods work best for them. Think of ways to train students to build on their own learning strengths so they can adjust conditions to suit them. As a student teacher, you should be assisting students in becoming more comfortable with several learning styles.

1. Review your students to see who learns primarily by each style:

   ____ auditory ____ visual ____ hands-on ____ random

   ____ sequential ____ inductive ____ deductive

   Most students are a combination of several but have a preferred approach.

2. Interview several students in the classroom about their preferred learning style. Ask each student why he or she prefers this style. If a student uses a combination, list them.

   Student *Preferred Style(s)* *Reason*

   ________________ ____

   ________________ ____

   ________________ ____

   ________________ ____

Establishing Routines

Routines are important for maintaining consistency and moving through a teaching day in a manner that students can expect. Routines can save valuable time and energy that can be put into academic areas. Routines can also be used to teach respect, to model expected behaviors, and to generally promote the positive attitude and environment you are seeking to create in the classroom.

As you observe or discuss routines with your mentor teacher, think about the following:

1. What is the purpose of the routine?
2. Are the students familiar with this routine? How do you know?
3. How does your mentor teacher reinforce a routine already established?
4. How does your mentor teacher present a new routine to the class?
5. What other skill(s) are students learning while participating in this routine?
6. Are routines saving time that can be used for teaching?

Routine Categories and Examples

A. Examples of *Opening Routines*
- Attendance and how to handle students who are absent so they get work
- Lunch count
- Collecting homework and recording it

B. Examples of *Operating Procedures*
- Walking to classes
- Leaving during class time
- Fire drills

C. Examples of *Teaching Routines*
- Expected behavior in classroom
- Class discussion procedures for listening to others
- Noise level for group work
- Students who forget books or materials
- What students do who finish early

D. Examples of *Closing Routines*
- Collecting work
- Leaving classroom
- Cleaning up

List other routines you observed.

What have you learned about routines and their affect on the classroom learning environment?

Rules, Rewards, and Consequences

Discuss ways rules are created in this school and in the various classrooms. How do rules, rewards, and consequences contribute to establishing a community of learners?

Work with your new teachers to establish systems that are fair and equitable to all students.

1. What are some ground rules that are fair and that work for you as a mentor?

2. How do you let students know what the consequences are *prior* to their breaking a rule?

3. What is your best advice to a new teacher who is setting up a classroom for the first time?

Invite the new teachers to share:

1. What are their problems, issues, concerns about this topic?

2. How they are establishing ground rules and what is working for them?

3. What they are noticing about rules for different grade levels?

Discuss how the school and district rules relate to teacher classroom rules.

First Month of School Issues

Share things that you may not have covered at the orientation.

How to . . .

- Sign out books from the resource center or library
- Use AV equipment—where to get it and how to sign it out
- Reserve books for class lessons
- Get all paper and school supplies
- Deal with medical emergencies
- Access student records
- Call for a substitute and leave work for the day

Procedures . . .

- Before school; entering the building
- Homeroom and cafeteria protocols
- Recess, snack time, and bus duty
- Study hall and paperwork

Space . . .

- Faculty-only rooms
- Students and faculty rooms
- Lunchrooms for faculty
- Meeting rooms
- Storage closets
- Book rooms
- Supply rooms

Using an aide or paraprofessional in the classroom

Writing notes to parents

Classroom and Behavior Management Issues

Classroom Routines and Organization

1. Review what your new teachers are doing in their classrooms to organize their space, time, and materials. Allow them to share their systems with you and each other. What is working for them?
2. Share effective systems that work for you for correcting papers, organizing materials, and grading student work. Focus on routines that save time and that may have taken years for you to figure out. Let them know that they don't need to reinvent the wheel. Don't dictate ideas and expect them all to be followed. Allow the new teachers to select the ones that fit for them and have that be OK with you.
3. Create a schedule that allows new teachers to talk with other teachers who have great ideas for organizing the classroom and their lessons.
4. Take time to discuss ways to begin and end lessons so that housekeeping activities required (such as collecting lunch money or homework) take minimal time away from classroom instruction.

Behavior Issues with Individual Students or the Whole Class

1. Ask new teachers if they are having any problems right now. If you are working with a small group of new teachers, take one of the problems and work together to give the groups some suggestions regarding possible solutions.
2. Connect new teachers with other teachers in the building who have creative ways to avoid behavior problems.
3. Discuss appropriate disciplinary actions for situations that arise. Discuss the difference between students not completing homework and students who are seriously disrespectful to others or to the new teachers.

Looking at Student Work

Invite the new teachers to bring samples of student work to a meeting. Have them select three students from the class randomly (without looking at names). If they created a rubric, have them bring that also.

1. Ask the new teachers what they notice about the completed work. Compare and contrast papers.
   Which students met the objective of the assignment?

   How do you know?

   Which students did not? Where do they fit on the rubric?

   How do you know?

2. Rate the papers using the rubric. If the new teachers do not have rubrics, create one together.
   List the rubric indicators:

1 meets criteria	2 meets most criteria	3 meets some criteria	4 meets few criteria	5 does not meet criteria

3. What is difficult about looking at student work?

4. Why is this important to review each month with the new teachers?

5. How skilled are you as a mentor in looking at student work? What is your next step?

Communicating with Parents

Discuss ways the new teachers should consider communicating with parents in September.

Examples may include:

- *A letter mailed to the home:* Share samples of letters that have been sent to parents from you or other teachers in the school. If the school sends a formal letter welcoming students, give the new teachers a copy. Some teachers also write a letter directly to the students, too.
- A *letter sent via the students:* It may be easier to write a letter and give it to the students to hand deliver to the parents sometime during the first week of school. New teachers may want to have a return receipt to ensure the parents or guardians received the communication.
- *An email to parents:* Some school systems even have parent communication through email. If this is an option at your school, share the appropriate ways to do this. The down side for email is that the parents then have access to the new teachers 24 hours a day, and this may be overwhelming for a new teacher.

Letters could include a brief biography of the new teacher, welcoming phrases, some examples of what the curriculum will include, and ways the parents can keep in touch. Policies for homework and expectations for materials students should bring to class may also be included.

Classroom Open House

Another way to connect with parents is to hold a classroom open house. Invite the parents in for "coffee and conversation" early in the morning before students arrive. Let them see the classroom and meet the new teacher in person.

Discuss Why It Is Important to Connect with Parents before There Are Behavior Issues with Any Students

- Sets up a relationship with the teacher that is professional.
- Demonstrates that the teacher is reaching out to share what is going on in the classroom.
- Allows the teacher to share expectations for learning and homework and gain support.
- Based on the response from parents, teachers get an indication of who is willing and able to connect—e.g., those parents who may not speak English, parents who work night shifts and can't attend meetings. This gives the new teacher time to create alternate ways to communicate throughout the school year.

New Teacher Needs

Review the Plan page in the beginning of this chapter, "What is needed and wanted?" by your new teachers. Create your own Activity for a discussion topic and set aside time to address this issue with your new teacher(s).

What is needed by your new teachers that was not included in the Activities list this month?

How can you help the new teacher in this area?

To whom can you refer the new teacher for additional support?

Each chapter lists a variety of common issues listed as Activities for discussion. As the mentor, you will need to select the most appropriate ones that relate to your new teachers' needs. In all chapters you have the opportunity to create your own discussion topic. Use this page as a guide in future months.

REFLECT *on This Month's Discussions*

Mentor's Reflections

Directions: Complete as many of the bubble prompts as you would like after you have finished the Activites in the chapter and before you Set Goals. Add your own prompts to blank bubbles if these prompts do not meet your needs. Ask your new teachers to complete their own reflection bubbles on the next page. Compare and share your reflections at one of your meetings. You may consider using one or two reflection bubbles as topics for future mentoring discussions.

Something I learned from my new teacher . . .
A goal we need to work on is . . .
Something I would like to work on together . . .
Questions I have . . .

New Teacher's Reflections

Directions: Complete as many of the bubble prompts as you would like after you have finished the Activities in the chapter and before you Set Goals. Add your own prompts to blank bubbles if the prompts listed do not meet your needs. Compare and share your reflections with your mentor and other new teachers at a scheduled meeting.

● SET GOALS *for Next Month*

Directions:

- Complete this Set Goals page the last day of the month after your Reflection and use it to guide the first week meeting for next month.
- Review the PLAN–CONNECT–ACT pages you completed in this chapter to see what you need to revisit next month based on the new teachers' needs. List two needs that stand out for you right now.
- Ask yourself how you would like to share what the new teachers need with them.

  Will you give a tour of your classroom?

  Will you share materials you have made?

  Will you take them to the library and show them how to use existing resources?

  Will you connect them with people who can assist them regularly?

  What will you do to be an effective mentor?
- List two goals for yourself as a mentor for next month. How do your goals relate to what observe the new teachers' top two needs to be?

New Teacher Needs (from reflections, conversations, and your observations)	**Your Mentor Goals**
1.	1.
2.	2.

October

A good teacher walks around the classroom helping everyone do things they don't understand. —Seventh-Grade Student

Teaching for Understanding

Planning and Delivering Effective Instruction

New Teacher Phase: Overwhelmed

"There is so much to do in one day!"

INTASC Principles

Introduce the new teacher to INTASC Principles 1 and 7.

- **PRINCIPLE 1 Making Content Meaningful**
  The teacher understands the central concepts, tools of inquiry, and structures of the discipline(s) he or she teaches and creates learning experiences that make these aspects of subject matter meaningful for students.
- **PRINCIPLE 7 Planning for Instruction**
  The teacher plans instruction based upon knowledge of subject matter, students, the community, and curriculum goals.

Teaching for Understanding

Planning and Delivering Effective Instruction

Getting through the first two months of school for any new teacher takes energy and lots of support. As the mentor, you can provide a safe place for the new teachers to talk and share what is really happening in their classrooms. Some new teachers may be overwhelmed by the amount of work they need to accomplish in any given day.

Use this month to talk about teaching expectations and curriculum. It is all about what students know and are able to do. Assist the new teachers in understanding the curriculum. Many of them may not have taught this, and it takes time to learn the content. Make time in your meetings for discussing content. Ask new teachers questions like the ones on the next page to assess how much they already know.

Try to assist them in uncovering what they do know instead of focusing on what they don't know. Most new teachers bring expertise into the classroom. Find out what that expertise is and acknowledge them for that! Computer skills are especially important in teaching, and new teachers usually have a command of new programs and ways to use technology in the classroom. Let the new teachers do a show-and-tell for the experienced teachers.

Every month there will be an opportunity to discuss recurring issues organized around the topics of Classroom and Behavior Management, Looking at Student Work, and Communicating with Parents. Use these pages as a springboard to discussions relevant to your new teachers.

Use the pages this month to . . . Plan your monthly meetings by deciding what you would like to talk about as well as to set meeting dates for the month, think about how you will Connect your new teachers to available resources, select Activities that make sense for you to discuss, Reflect at the end of the month, and Set Goals for next month. Use all of these process pages as a guide to enrich the quality of your monthly mentoring conversations.

What Do We Want to Talk about When We Meet This Month?

Invite your new teachers to write down a short list of questions and bring them to your first meeting in October. Use the questions below as a guide for your discussions throughout the month.

New Teachers' Possible Questions:

1. What does the district expect of me as a first-year teacher?
2. How can I learn the district curriculum and goals?
3. How do I make content meaningful when I have the test scores as outcomes of success?
4. How much planning do I have to do? Are my plans reviewed by the principal?
5. Will I be observed this month?
6. How can I backwards plan so I can get through the content in a timely way?
7. Can you give me some successful strategies for engaging learners in interactive ways that won't lead to misbehavior?

List the other questions your new teachers brought to the meeting below so you will have them for your next mentoring cycle.

As a Mentor, You Can Ask Questions, Too!

Try to ask more questions to learn about your new teachers, rather than telling them how things should be done.

Mentor's Possible Questions:

1. What do you know about teaching for understanding? Have you taken a course that covers this topic?
2. What do you already know about our district goals and curriculum?
3. How do you like teachers to make content meaningful for you as a student?
4. What can I do to assist you right now that would reduce your anxiety?

● PLAN *Agendas and Schedule Meetings*

Plan your monthly meetings, decide when and how you want to Connect with each other as well as others in the school and community, select the Activities from this chapter that make sense for you to discuss, Reflect separately at the end of the end of the month and share your reflection, and Set Goals for next month.

PLAN *Agendas for Monthly Meetings Based on New Teacher Needs*

Planning quality conversations means that the needs of the new teacher must be met. Take time to complete the chart before making decisions about what you will discuss at your monthly mentoring sessions. What makes most sense for you as a mentor to share in October?

Complete this together and save for future discussion. Make a copy for each new teacher if needed.

What is needed and wanted in October?

New Teacher *I need . . .*	Mentor *I want to share . . .*

When Will We Meet?

Plan to meet at times that allow you to have quality time together without interruptions. Knowing when you will meet reduces anxiety for both of you all month. New teachers look forward to planned meetings.

When will you meet?

How many times during the month?

How long will you meet for quality conversations? Ten, twenty, or thirty minutes? Indicate that on this calendar.

Will your new teacher observe you teach and demonstrate a skill this month?

Will you observe the new teachers this month? Purpose of the observation is . . .

Are there other teachers or community members your new teachers need to connect with this month? Indicate on this schedule.

Make a copy of this calendar for each new teacher. Also put these times into your teaching plan book.

October Calendar

MONDAY	TUESDAY	WEDNESDAY	THURSDAY	FRIDAY

Key: B = before school D = during the day (preparation time or lunch time) A = After school

● CONNECT *with People, Readings, Professional Associations, Resources, and Technology*

What resources exist in your school and community that could assist new teachers in teaching for understanding?

Directions:

1. Review the answers you both completed in the "What is needed and wanted?" boxes on page 72. What does the new teacher need? What do you want to share? Keep the answers to these questions in mind when you explore possible resources.
2. Copy this Connect page so you both can investigate resources separately. Bring your completed October Plan "What is needed and wanted?" and Connect pages to the next meeting and compare what you both discovered. If you are working with a group of new teachers, make copies of all of their completed Connect pages and distribute the resource ideas to everyone in the group.

CONNECT *with People . . .*

Who in the school building (experienced teachers, other beginning teachers, custodians, secretaries, etc.) may be able to help with October needs?

What agencies in the community relate to the topic of "teaching for understanding"?

How can parents be helpful in making content more meaningful to students?

CONNECT *with Readings, Professional Associations, and Resources . . .*

What have you read or used that would assist in making content meaningful and planning effective lessons? New teachers may refer to student teaching courses and readings. Mentors may have books that relate to this topic.

CONNECT *with Technology . . .*

Find websites and links that will provide information about:

- Teaching for understanding
- Making content meaningful at ______ grade level
- Lesson plans that relate to district curriculum topics
- Teaching in the content area(s) websites

● ACTIVITIES: *Select Topics for Quality Discussions*

What Will We Discuss at Our October Meetings?

Each month begins with a formal first week planning meeting where dates and times for discussions are scheduled. Use the agenda in this chapter to guide your meeting. Select Activity pages listed on this page as possible talking points at this meeting or for any other meetings you schedule during the month. Record your meeting dates and time on your Planning Calendar. You may decide to assign some Activity pages to the new teacher for completion alone. Use the Appendix for five-, ten-, fifteen-, twenty-, thirty-, and sixty-minute meeting formats you may want to use during the month.

Schedule this meeting during the first week of the month	**PLAN the Monthly Discussions (see sample agenda)**
✓ The Activities you will discuss	**ACT by Selecting Appropriate Topics for Discussions during the Month**
	Activities for October discussions related to *Teaching for Understanding* include . . .
	ACT 1 Planning the Lesson Plan
	ACT 2 Planning for Understanding
	ACT 3 What Should the Students Know and Be Able to Do?
	ACT 4 Engaging Students in Meaningful Learning Experiences
	ACT 5 Pacing a Lesson
	ACT 6 Organizing a Lesson
	ACT 7 Designing a Unit
	ACT 8 A Unit Organizer
	* ACT 9 Classroom and Behavior Management Issues
	* ACT 10 Looking at Student Work
	* ACT 11 Communicating with Parents
The last day of the month the new teachers and you complete these pages on your own.	**REFLECT and SET GOALS for Next Month** **Give new teachers copies of REFLECT and SET GOALS pages to bring to the November first week meeting.**

*These three Activities will be offered each month.

First Week Agenda: Making a Plan for the Month

TOPIC: Teaching for Understanding: Planning and Delivering Effective Instruction

Have snacks and water or soft drinks available. Hold the meeting in your classroom or another comfortable space where you will be sure you will not be interrupted. Put a colorful sign on your door that says "Mentoring Meeting—Please do not disturb."

First: Welcome and introductions: Invite new teachers to share something that is going well.

Then: Review the September new teacher Reflections.

- How did the new teachers respond? How will this impact what you do next?
- Share any of your mentor Reflections that are appropriate.

Next: Review the Set Goals page that you both completed the last day of September.

- How will these goals carry over into this month?
- What do we want to talk about when we meet this month?
- Share the possible key questions listed at the beginning of this chapter.
- What most interests the new teachers right now?

Begin: Plan what you will discuss this month use the Planning calendar to set your meeting times. Think about how you should share information with the new teachers. Will you give handouts, a tour of your room, or hold discussions? Review the Activities pages for handouts and discussion ideas. Use the Appendix for five-, ten-, fifteen-, twenty-, thirty-, and sixty-minute meeting templates. Modify Activities and templates as needed.

Network: Complete the Connections page together.

Acknowledge: Recognize what you and the new teachers have done so far instead of focusing on what they don't know. Remind the new teachers that they will complete Reflections and Set Goals pages on their own the last day of the month to bring to the first week meeting the next month.

Share: End the session with compliments for each new teacher and at least one practical idea related to planning and delivering lessons. Let new teachers share ideas with each other, too.

Creating the Lesson Plan

Discuss the following questions with your new teachers. Invite them to bring copies of lesson plans they are creating. Bring samples of your own lesson plans.

- *Why am I teaching this lesson?* required curriculum? student interest? new teacher interest? other?
- *What do I hope to accomplish?* skill development? concept to be discussed for understanding? product to be produced?
- *Who are the students?* range of abilities? range of ages? ethnic diversity and varying cultures?
- *What is the time frame for teaching this lesson?* part of a unit? one period or block schedule? isolated lesson?
- *How will I begin the lesson to capture student attention?* story, anecdote? relevance to their lives? props or visual displays?
- *Will I need other resources to teach this lesson?* audiovisual or technology? student handouts? manipulatives or visual displays?
- *How will students spend their time during the lesson?* small-group discussion? individual? large group? hands-on activity or experiment? taking notes or observing?
- *How will this lesson be assessed?* formal? quiz or test? informal? observation of learning? open-ended questions? written? verbal?
- *How will I close the lesson and close the class period?* review and summary? collecting papers? giving next assignment? allowing time for homework or questions?
- *Will there be homework or enrichment activities offered?* how will I collect later? is it required or extra? will it count? what is cooperating teacher's policy? how will I grade it?
- *How will I know whether I succeeded in teaching the lesson?* self-assessment? response of students? cooperating teacher input?
- *How will the next lesson relate to or build on this one?*

Planning for Understanding

A teacher knows he or she has a good plan when at the end of the lesson or unit there is evidence of student understanding or skill development. An effective teacher, like an architect, designs a plan that will create a solid foundation for creative and original thinking. Teachers present information not just to be memorized for the weekly test, but to be understood and integrated into a student's thinking. This is not an easy task, but one that should be kept in your awareness as you begin to plan lessons.

What do you want students to know, understand, and be able to do *as a result of your lesson?*

Four Steps to Meaningful Lesson Planning

1. *Think about breadth or depth* as you design your lessons and units.
   Are you aiming for breadth in your lessons, e.g., being able to connect this concept to other concepts or relevant experiences?
   - Students explain why or why not
   - Students extend the concept to others
   - Students think about and give examples of similar concepts

   Are you aiming for depth in your lessons, i.e., looking more at the detail about this idea?
   - Students question the information
   - Students analyze the facts
   - Students prove something
2. *Set priorities* for assessing student growth in lessons and units.
   What do you expect all students to be familiar with?
   - to be able to do in this class?
   - to really understand for lasting learning?
3. *Select measurement tools* to determine student understanding.
   How will you know students understand?
   - What do *all* students have to know? How will you know?
   - What do *most* students have to know? How will you know?
   - What will *some* students have to know? How will you know?
4. *Create meaningful learning experiences* that engage and support learning (not just busywork).
   - MOTIVATE—Have you included a "hook" to gain attention and provide relevance?
   - QUESTIONS—Do you have key questions that promote discussion and thinking?
   - PRACTICE—Do you have time for students to practice and engage in activity?
   - SELF-ASSESSMENT—Do you allow students time to reflect on their work and set goals?

What Should the Students Know and Be Able to Do?

Objectives state what the teacher wants the students to accomplish on completion of the lesson. Students should be clear about objectives before they begin the lesson so they know what is expected of them. Objectives should be written as one sentence.

Use verbs to write your lesson plan objectives. *Bloom's Taxonomy* organizes the verbs by levels of understanding, beginning with basic knowledge and moving up through comprehension, application, analysis, synthesis, and evaluation. Higher level thinking is expected for verbs at levels 5 and 6. These verbs indicate what the student should be doing.

As you write your lesson plan objectives, select a verb and complete the sentence to state what is to be accomplished. State the objective in clear terms that can easily be understood by students and parents. Be sure to vary the levels of complexity in your lessons.

Examples: Name the planets, in order from the sun.
Predict the ending to this story.
Explain the reasons for the start of the Civil War.

Level of Understanding	Example Verbs
6 Evaluation	choose, conclude, evaluate, defend, rank, support, rate
5 Synthesis	construct, create, formulate, revise, write, plan, predict
4 Analysis	analyze, classify, compare, contrast, debate, categorize
3 Application	apply, demonstrate, draw, show, solve, illustrate
2 Comprehension	describe, explain, paraphrase, summarize, rewrite
1 Knowledge	define, identify, label, list, memorize, spell, name

What do you, in the role of the teacher, need to do to have the students experience a variety of learning objectives at all levels?

Remember, an effective teacher teaches so students meet the objectives stated in the lesson plan.

Engaging Students in Meaningful Learning Experiences

How does an effective teacher initially gain students' attention to shift from noninstructional announcements to instructional curriculum? Does he or she use a story? A prop? A question? Does he or she connect what is coming up in the lesson to the students' own experiences?

List any ways teachers motivate and gain attention:

____

____

The Lesson

How does an effective teacher maintain this attention if there is a whole class? If there are small groups, is it different? How does he or she ensure all students are engaged in a learning experience? Does he or she walk around? How does he or she interact with students to keep them on task? Does he or she call on students?

List any "maintaining" management strategies you have observed:

____

____

Closing the Lesson/Ending the Class Period

How does an effective teacher complete the lesson? How does he or she know the students learned? How does he or she check for understanding? Are there non-instructional directions that need to be given at the end of class? Is there time for questions and answers, or does the lesson just end? Is there time for students to do homework? How does the teacher close the lesson and end the class period? How are these things different?

List the management techniques for closing you have observed:

____

____

How does opening, maintaining, and closing a lesson in a predictable and organized way contribute to student learning?

Pacing a Lesson

One of the biggest concerns teachers have about teaching is that they don't have enough time in the day to do all there is to do. The majority of the time spent in class should be on teaching the curriculum that you have planned, not on making announcements, collecting lunch money, passing out materials, getting students into groups, or cleaning up. However, these tasks do need to get done.

A class period is your "allocated teaching time," but it also needs to include housekeeping activities. "Instructional time" is the time when students are actually engaged in learning activities. Your lesson plan is the way to organize your thinking so that most of the allocated time is spent engaging students in learning and checking for understanding.

Allocated Class Time: How Much Should You Spend?		
How much time?	Starting Class Period Housekeeping Activities	• Required tasks • Collection of homework
Time?	BEGINNING LESSON Introducing or connecting to previous day	• Motivation/relevance • Overview • Directions • Purpose of lesson
Time?	MIDDLE	• Objective • Key questions • Students engaged in learning • Activity • Knowledge • Student sharing • Informal assessment and checking for understanding
Time?	CLOSING	• Wrap up • Review of key points • Collection of materials/papers
Time?	Ending Class Period Housekeeping Activities	• Required tasks • Collection of classwork

Use this as a guide and include time as a factor in designing your lesson plans. When you have a particularly complicated lesson with many materials or if you need to move students into groups, take that into consideration and think of ways to prepare and set up so you don't take away from teaching time.

Organizing a Lesson

Lesson plan title: *Write the name of the topic or class here* **Date:** *Day you teach lesson*

Time of class: *Period or time* **Length of period:** *How much time to teach*

Subject: *Content*

Purpose of lesson: *Why are you teaching this lesson? What goal are you seeking to reach ?*

Objective: *Bloom's taxonomy verb—what the student will achieve or accomplish*

Theme or unit #___: *Is this an isolated lesson or part of a bigger curriculum unit? Number it as to where it fits in the sequence. If there is an expectation that students need prior knowledge to complete the lesson, how will you handle this with new students or those who have missed?*

Key questions: *The questions you will introduce to the students to guide the discussion and activities of the lesson should be broadly designed to encourage discussion and critical thinking. (Questions should not be designed with a yes or no answer.)*

Procedure: *Note that the class period includes other housekeeping activities, such as collecting papers from the night before, announcing future school activities, or collecting lunch money. These need to be incorporated into the lesson plan to avoid running out of teaching time.*

Sample Procedure for Use of Allotted Classroom Time

Time	Classroom Lesson	Teacher Behaviors: What will you be doing?	Expected Student Behaviors: What will the students be doing?
5%	Starting Class Period	Housekeeping	Listening Passing in homework
10%	Beginning Lesson	Introducing objectives, vocabulary, and key questions	Showing interest Participating, listening
70%	Middle of Lesson	Facilitating a variety of activities for student learning	Collaborating Thinking, discussing Responding to key questions
10%	Closing Lesson	Summarizing and reviewing lesson Setting goals for next lesson	Answering key questions Self-assessing
5%	Ending Class Period	Housekeeping	Passing in materials

Designing a Unit

A unit is an organized group of lesson plans with a beginning, various activities, and a culmination. The unit may be subject-based, interdisciplinary, or thematic. It can last as long as a semester or as short as a week. It has overarching themes and concepts to be learned through daily lessons. Teachers typically organize their teaching in units by skills for early childhood, by subjects or themes for elementary/middle, or by subject area topics at secondary levels. Units are organized around books students have read, historical events, science themes, topics, or anything teachers can think of that relates to knowledge.

A unit will have a general outline or plan for implementation and the daily lesson plans that demonstrate in detail how the plan is to be carried out in the classroom. Lesson plans are created as you move through the unit, not ahead of time, because the original plan often changes.

Questions to Consider before Beginning a Unit

- What is the purpose of the unit?
- How much time will the unit need? How many lessons?
- What do students already know?
- What would students like to learn or know?
- How will the unit be introduced?
- What are the key questions that need to be answered?
- Is prior knowledge necessary?
- Will the unit have a theme?
- Will the unit cross disciplines? Is team teaching involved?
- Will any special activities be part of the unit?
- Will I need special materials or audiovisual for this unit?
- Will guest speakers or field trips be part of the unit?
- Other?

A Unit Organizer

One example is . . .

Title of Unit				
Purpose	Objectives	Key Questions	Key Vocabulary	Materials
Assessments	Possible Daily Lesson Activities	Opening Activity	Culmination	Guests or Trips

Classroom and Behavior Management Issues

Before disciplining a student, ask your new teachers to ask themselves . . .

- ☐ Who is the student?

  Does this student have a prearranged plan when disruptive? For example, sent to guidance, principal, or resource or learning center classroom?

  Is this a first offense or is this repeated misbehavior?

  Does this student have a special need that has not been addressed?

  Are there other adults who need to be notified when this student is disruptive?

- ☐ What rule did the student break?

  Is it a major offense? For example, hitting someone or possessing a weapon.

  Is it a minor offense? For example, chewing gum or wearing a hat.

  Is it related to academic work? For example, not doing homework or cheating.

  Is it related to work habits? For example, not listening in class.

- ☐ What did the student specifically do or say?

- ☐ Is this misbehavior appropriate for the student's age?

- ☐ Where did the misbehavior take place?

  In classroom?

  On playground, hallway, cafeteria, en route to class?

  Off school grounds but near school?

- ☐ Is this behavior a common occurrence?

  For this student?

  For others in the school?

- ☐ Do you have personal feelings about this student?

  Have you interacted positively or negatively before this?

  Do you know this student at all?

- ☐ What are your legal rights when dealing with disruptive students?

  State and local guidelines for restraining students, searching lockers, etc.?

  School policies related to alcohol, drugs, weapons?

  Students with educational plans?

Notes:

Looking at Student Work

Ask new teachers to bring several samples of student work to a meeting. In pairs have them look at student work and analyze it for:

Standards:

What was the objective of this work?

What was the student supposed to accomplish?

Quality:

What did the work look like?

Was the student proud of this work?

Expectations:

What did you expect the student to do on this assignment?

Are your expectations limiting the student's achievement?

Discuss the importance of looking at student work systematically.

Communicating with Parents

Letting Parents Know What New Teachers Are Teaching

Discuss possible ways your new teachers can let parents know about the curriculum and the routines of your classroom. Parents often ask their children, "What did you do in school today?" Students respond, "Nothing!" We all know that is not true. As a mentor, you can encourage the new teachers with whom you are working to be proactive in communicating with the parents of their students. Often communication comes when there is a problem and then parents are on the defensive. Share positive ways to connect with parents.

Newsletters

Why not put the students to work and have them write short articles about the lessons they are learning in school and turn it into a newsletter for parents? New teachers can use this as a learning experience for students while informing parents. *Education Matters!* could be the name of the newsletter, or students could vote on a name they like. Students can hand deliver the newsletter or it could be mailed directly to the parents.

Classroom Open House

Another way to new teachers can connect with parents and share what is going in the classroom is to host an open house in the classroom. Invite the parents in for "coffee and conversation" early in the morning before students arrive or include students. Share the logistics of this type of event with the new teachers. Brainstorm ways students can show off their work and how new teachers can let parents know how they can help their children progress.

Classroom Web Page

Many teachers entering the profession have technology skills and are able to create web pages. If your school and district have the capabilities for a web-based newsletter, encourage the new teachers to do it. It is a fun and easy way to get the parents' attention!

Cable TV Show

Another option for sharing what is going on could be a classroom TV show. Let students produce and direct a show that lets parents know what they are learning. New teachers may not have time for one on their own, but perhaps several could get together and put on short segments. It would also be a great way to introduce the new teachers to the school district!

• REFLECT *on This Month's Discussions*

Mentor's Reflections

Directions: Complete as many of the bubble prompts as you would like after you have finished the Activites in the chapter and before you Set Goals. Add your own prompts to blank bubbles if these prompts do not meet your needs. Ask your new teachers to complete their own reflection bubbles on the next page. Compare and share your reflections at one of your meetings. You may consider using one or two reflection bubbles as topics for future mentoring discussions.

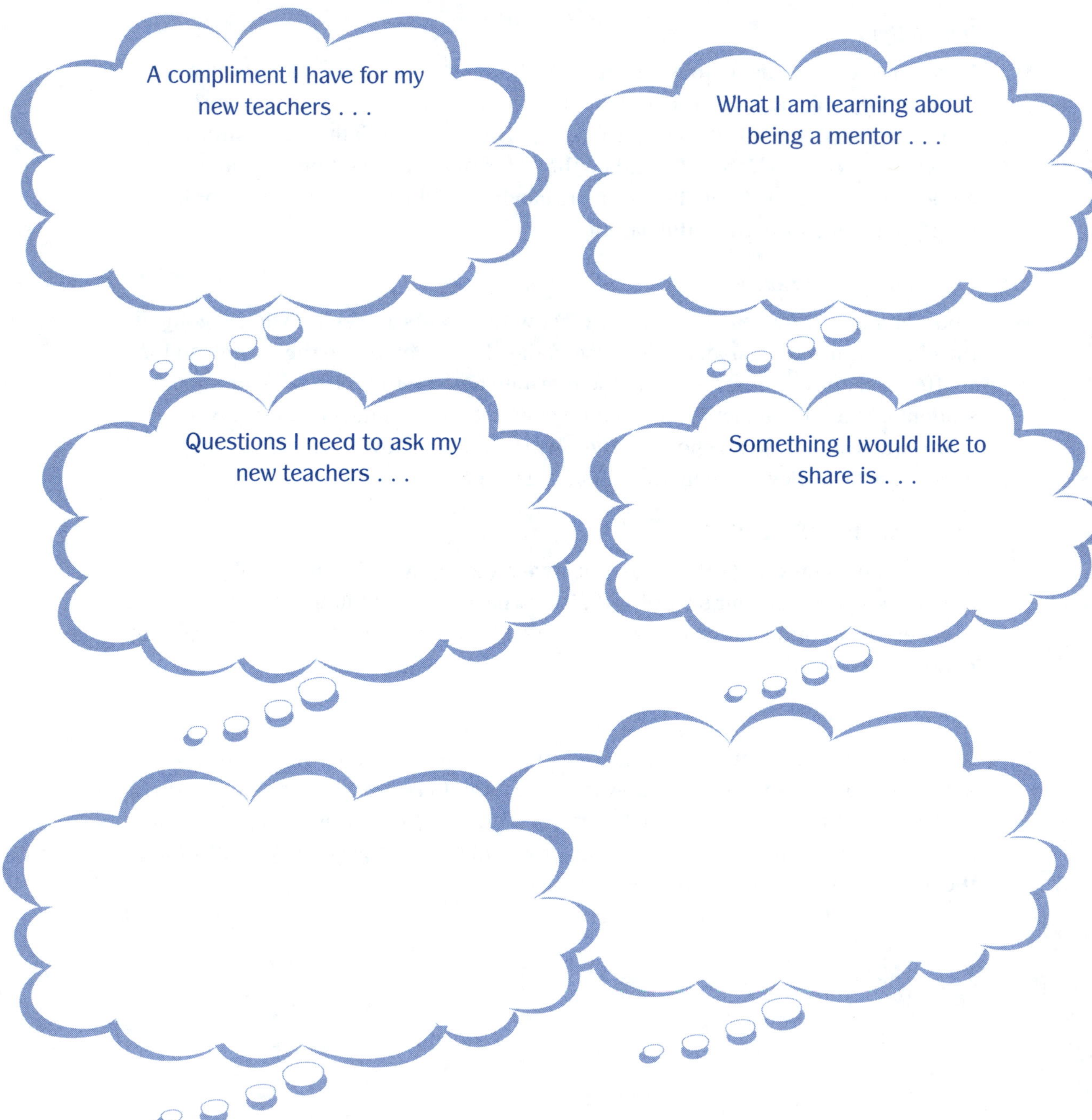

A compliment I have for my new teachers . . .
What I am learning about being a mentor . . .
Questions I need to ask my new teachers . . .
Something I would like to share is . . .

New Teachers' Reflections

Directions: Complete as many of the bubble prompts as you would like after you have finished the Activites in the chapter and before you Set Goals. Add your own prompts to blank bubbles if the prompts listed do not meet your needs. Compare and share your reflections with your mentor and other new teachers at a scheduled meeting.

SET GOALS *for Next Month*

Directions:

- Complete this Set Goals page the last day of the month after your Reflection and use it to guide the first week meeting for next month.
- Review the PLAN–CONNECT–ACT pages you completed in this chapter to see what you need to revisit next month based on the new teachers' needs. List two needs that stand out for you right now.
- Ask yourself how you would like to share what the new teachers need with them.

  Will you give a tour of your classroom?

  Will you share materials you have made?

  Will you take them to the library and show them how to use existing resources?

  Will you connect them with people who can assist them regularly?

  What will you do to be an effective mentor?
- List two goals for yourself as a mentor for next month. How do your goals relate to what observe the new teachers' top two needs to be?

New Teacher Needs (from reflections, conversations, and your observations)	Your Mentor Goals
1.	1.
2.	2.

November

I know I have learned something when I have the confidence to do it alone. —Fourth-Grade Student

Assessing Diverse Learners

How Do Teachers Know Students Have Learned?

New Teacher Phase: Disillusioned

"I'm not sure if I made the right choice to teach. This is really hard."

INTASC Principles

Introduce the new teacher to INTASC Principles 3 and 8.

- **PRINCIPLE 3 Learning Styles/Diversity**
  The teacher understands how students differ in their approaches to learning and creates instructional opportunities that are adapted to diverse learners.
- **PRINCIPLE 8 Assessment**
  The teacher understands and uses formal and informal assessment strategies to evaluate and ensure the continuous intellectual, social, and physical development of the learner.

Assessing Diverse Learners

How Do Teachers Know Students Have Learned?

New teachers need to be competent and have confidence in what they are doing. They may arrive idealistic and full of ideas, but by November some are disillusioned and question whether they can do this at all. As a mentor, you can provide nurturing and support that lets them know this is a normal phase of teaching. In fact, some veteran teachers are disillusioned in November!

Students need teachers who allow them to learn content so well they can do it on their own. Like the fourth-grade student's quote on the first page of this chapter, "I know I have learned something when I have the confidence to do it alone." In some ways this is like the new teachers with whom you are working. They may need you to answer questions and assist this year, but your goal is to help them find their confidence. Confidence leads to more competence. Competence in teaching then leads to more confidence. New teachers are learners, just as their students are this year. Assessing how much students learn will be a parallel process to assessing how much the new teachers are learning.

Use the Activities in the chapter to discuss important ways the new teachers can tap into students' prior knowledge and monitor their progress. Tap into the new teachers' prior knowledge by asking them questions, like the ones on page 93, and by letting them select the Activities they need to focus on this month.

Learning styles of students in their classrooms will impact the assessments these new teachers should use to measure growth. Think about your role in guiding a new teacher in learning how to assess diverse learners. Remember that the new teachers have their own learning styles, teaching styles, and diversity. How will you accommodate their needs in different ways? Mentoring is a lot like teaching.

Use the pages this month to . . . Plan your monthly meetings by deciding what you would like to talk about as well as to set meeting dates for the month, think about how you will Connect your new teachers to available resources, select Activities that make sense for you to discuss, Reflect at the end of the month, and Set Goals for next month. Use all of these process pages as a guide to enrich the quality of your monthly mentoring conversations.

What Do We Want to Talk about When We Meet This Month?

Invite you new teacher(s) to write down a short list of questions and bring them to your first November meeting. Use the questions below as a guide for your discussions throughout the month.

New Teachers' Possible Questions:

1. Who are my students (languages, learning styles, special needs, learning modifications, family background, etc.)?
2. What do I need to know about their parents that will assist me?
3. How can I set up my lessons and learning to adapt for the needs of my diverse learners?
4. What high stakes formal assessments are a part of district expectations?
5. What formal assessments should I be creating or using this year?
6. Can you review informal assessment with me and share where you think I should be doing it?

List the other questions your new teachers brought to the meeting so you will have them for your next mentoring cycle.

As a Mentor, You Can Ask Questions, Too!

Try to ask more questions to learn about your new teachers, rather than telling them how things should be done.

Mentor's Possible Questions:

1. What do you already know about tests and assessment?
2. What do you already know about teaching diverse learners?
3. Share one strategy you have used that assisted a student who was struggling to learn new information.
4. What can I do to assist you right now that would reduce your anxiety?

PLAN *Agendas and Schedule Meetings*

Plan your monthly meetings, decide when and how you want to Connect with each other as well as others in the school and community, select the Activities from this chapter that make sense for you to discuss, Reflect separately at the end of the end of the month and share your reflection, and Set Goals for next month.

PLAN *Agendas for Monthly Meetings Based on NewTeacher Needs*

Planning quality conversations means that the needs of the new teacher must be met. Take time to complete the chart before making decisions about what you will discuss at your monthly mentoring sessions. What makes most sense for you as a mentor to share in November?

Complete this together and save for future discussion. Make a copy for each new teacher if needed.

What is needed and wanted in November?

New Teacher *I need . . .*	Mentor *I want to share . . .*

When Will We Meet?

Plan to meet at times that allow you to have quality time together without interruptions. Knowing when you will meet reduces anxiety for both of you all month. New teachers look forward to planned meetings.

When will you meet?

How many times during the month?

How long will you meet for quality conversations? Ten, twenty, or thirty minutes? Indicate that on this calendar.

Will your new teacher observe you teach and demonstrate a skill this month?

Will you observe the new teachers this month? Purpose of the observation is . . .

Are there other teachers or community members your new teachers need to connect with this month? Indicate on this schedule.

Make a copy of this calendar for each new teacher. Also put these times into your teaching plan book.

November Calendar

MONDAY	TUESDAY	WEDNESDAY	THURSDAY	FRIDAY

Key: B = before school D = during the day (preparation time or lunch time) A = After school

CONNECT *with People, Readings, Professional Associations, Resources, and Technology*

What resources exist in your school and community that could assist new teachers in assessing diverse learners?

Directions:

1. Review the answers you both completed in the "What is needed and wanted?" boxes on page 94. What does the new teacher need? What do you want to share? Keep the answers to these questions in mind when you explore possible resources.
2. Copy this Connect page so you both can investigate resources separately. Bring your completed November Plan "What is needed and wanted?" and Connect pages to the next meeting and compare what you both discovered. If you are working with a group of new teachers, make copies of all of their completed Connect pages and distribute the resource ideas to everyone in the group.

CONNECT *with People . . .*

Who in the school building (experienced teachers, other beginning teachers, custodians, secretaries, etc.) may be able to help with November needs?

What agencies in the community relate to the topic of assessing diverse learners?

How can parents be helpful in having new teachers understand students' learning styles?

CONNECT *with Readings, Professional Associations, and Resources . . .*

What have you read or used that would assist in the areas of diversity, assessment, and learning styles? New teachers may refer to student teaching courses and readings. Mentors may have books that relate to these topics.

CONNECT *with Technology . . .*

Find websites and links that will provide information about:

- Learning styles and teaching styles
- Diverse learners
- Informal assessment strategies (search by grade levels and disciplines)
- Formal assessments
- High stakes tests for your state and district and No Child Left Behind Act

● ACTIVITIES: *Select Topics for Quality Discussions*

What Will We Discuss at Our November Meetings?

Each month begins with a formal first week planning meeting where dates and times for discussions are scheduled. Use the agenda in this chapter to guide your meeting. Select Activity pages listed on this page as possible talking points at this meeting or for any other meetings you schedule during the month. Record your meeting dates and time on your Planning calendar. You may decide to assign some Activity pages to the new teacher for completion alone. Use the Appendix for five-, ten-, fifteen-, twenty-, thirty-, and sixty-minute meeting formats you may want to use during the month.

Schedule this meeting during the first week of the month	**PLAN the Monthly Discussions (see sample agenda)**
✓ The Activities you will discuss	**ACT by Selecting Appropriate Topics for Discussions during the Month**
	Activities for November discussions related to *Assessment* include . . .
	ACT 1 How Are Students Assessed and Evaluated?
	ACT 2 Linking Lesson Plans to Assessment
	ACT 3 Tapping in to Students' Prior Knowledge
	ACT 4 A Variety of Ways to Observe Student Learning
	ACT 5 What Should Students Know and Be Able to Do?
	ACT 6 Formative and Summative Assessments
	ACT 7 Using Rubrics and Portfolios to Assess Performance
	ACT 8 Documenting Progress and Record Keeping Strategies
	ACT 9 Can Students Monitor Their Progress?
	ACT 10 Communicating with Students about Their Progress
	* ACT 11 Classroom and Behavior Management Issues
	* ACT 12 Looking at Student Work
	* ACT 13 Communicating with Parents
The last day of the month the new teachers and you complete these pages on your own.	**REFLECT and SET GOALS for Next Month** **Give new teachers copies of REFLECT and SET GOALS pages to bring to the December first week meeting.**

*These three Activities will be offered each month.

First Week Agenda: Making a Plan for the Month

TOPIC: Assessing Diverse Learners: How Do Teachers Know Students Have Learned?

Have snacks and water or soft drinks available. Hold the meeting in your classroom or another comfortable space where you will be sure you will not be interrupted. Put a colorful sign on your door that says "Mentoring Meeting—Please do not disturb."

First: Welcome and introductions: Invite new teachers to share something that is going well

Then: Review the October new teacher Reflections.

- How did the new teachers respond? How will this impact what you do next?
- Share any of your mentor Reflections that are appropriate.

Next: Review the Set Goals page that you both completed the last day of October.

- How will these goals carry over into this month?
- What do we want to talk about when we meet this month?
- Share the possible key questions listed at the beginning of this chapter.
- What most interests the new teachers right now?

Begin: Plan what you will discuss this month use the Planning calendar to set your meeting times. Think about how you should share information with the new teachers. Will you give handouts, a tour of your room, or hold discussions? Review the Activities pages for handouts and discussion ideas. Use the Appendix for five-, ten-, fifteen-, twenty-, thirty-, and sixty-minute meeting templates. Modify Activities and templates as needed.

Network: Complete the Connections page together.

Acknowledge: Recognize what you and the new teachers have done so far instead of focusing on what they don't know. Remind the new teachers that they will complete Reflections and Set Goals pages on their own the last day of the month to bring to the first week meeting the next month.

Share: End the session with compliments for each new teacher and at least one practical idea related to assessment. Let new teachers share ideas with each other, too.

How Are Students Assessed and Evaluated?

Share with your new teachers all the types of tests the students will take this year. Review the purposes of the tests and explain the procedures. Explain how all state and local tests relate to the environment for learning you are attempting to create with your students.

State Testing Initiatives

Does the state have a statewide testing program? What is its purpose?

Are the students required to pass a high school exit exam? When is it given? What is the test? Are there other state tests required? Which grade levels? Ask to review a copy of the tests if they are at your grade level.

On what standards or frameworks are the tests based? How will this state test affect the curriculum you teach in your classroom?

District Testing Program

What is the purpose of these tests?

Does the district require tests for certain grades? Note the test names here:

____

Are these tests similar to the state tests? How?

Classroom Assessment and Evaluation Procedures

How do you use *informal* assessment to assess learning? Journals? Notecards? File folders? Portfolios? Notes in rank book? Share all your strategies with your student teacher.

How do you *formally* assess students for understanding? Teacher-made tests? Publishing company tests? Performance assessment? Portfolios? Share all assessment tools with the new teachers.

Linking Lesson Plans to Assessment

Lesson planning and assessment are linked. Remind the new teachers that the lesson plan and assessment or evaluation of the lesson should be written at the same time. This ensures that students will be responding to the key questions and objectives established for learning. What do you want students to be able to do? What will students know as a result of this lesson?

Share a lesson plan you recently created with the new teachers. Were your objectives clear? Did you know what you wanted students to learn? What type of assessment did you create or do you need to create to measure student achievement? Did your assessment approach match your lesson's activities?

How do other teachers create forms of assessment in this school? Encourage the new teacher to talk with these teachers. They can share what they learned at your next meeting.

Tapping into Students' Prior Knowledge

An important aspect of assessment is knowing where students are before you begin teaching. Students come to the classroom with varied backgrounds and experience levels related to the topic you may be presenting. Being able to assess this knowledge as part of your regular planning process is important to designing lessons that meet the needs of the diverse learners in your classroom. ELL (English language learners) need support.

1. Share how experienced teachers have tapped into your prior knowledge.

2. How have you observed other teachers tapping into students' prior knowledge?

Ways to tap in . . .

- Ask students privately on paper before the lesson begins . . .
  What do you already know about this topic/skill?
  What do you think you know or have you heard about this topic/skill?
  What would you like to learn or know?
- Collect the papers. At the end of the unit or lesson ask what they learned and have them write it on the bottom of the sheet they had previously started.
- Give a pretest on the topic, testing for spelling words, math skill, and so on.
- Have students write a paragraph about what they know about the topic.

Tapping in can avoid teaching students who may already *know* the information. It also assists you in designing lessons to meet the current needs of your students.

Tapping in can also serve as a check-in toward the middle and near the end of the term to let you know how closely the lesson objectives are being met.

A Variety of Ways to Observe Student Learning

How do you observe student achievement? Will a product let you know that the student achieved the objectives or do you need to observe the student perform and demonstrate the skill or understanding of the topic? Explain the difference between *product* and *process* assessment to the new teachers. Remind them that the assessment/evaluation depends on the lesson's objective. Be sure the achievement measure matches the objective designed in the student teacher's lesson plan. Suggestions for product and process assessments include the following:

Product (paper/pencil)	Product (visual)	Performance Process (with or without product)
Essays	Posters	Oral reports
Book reports	Banners	Speeches
Biographies	Models	Raps
Journals	Diagrams	Dramatizations
Letters	Displays	Debates
Editorials	Videotapes or audiotapes	Songs
Scripts	Portfolios	Poems
Tests	Exhibits	Demonstrations
Research reports	Paintings	Interviews
Short answers	Photos	Skits
Position papers	Websites	News reports

Ask the new teachers to assess their lessons for the following:

Are your lessons always requiring the same type of assessment or evaluation?

Are you providing alternative assessments for all learners?

What Should Students Know and Be Able to Do?

1. As you discuss this topic, review the following concepts with your new teachers:

   - What should students be able to DO to show they understand?

     Write something?

     Respond to an open-ended question?

     Perform a skit?

     Understanding can be demonstrated by observing students explain, interpret, apply, persuade, create, design, defend, critique, correct, summarize, translate, compare, and contrast the information or skill in their own words.
   - What should all students be able to know or do at the end of a particular lesson or unit? How will you know whether they achieved that goal?
   - What would be important for *most* of them to know? How will you know?
   - What would be worth knowing for *some* students? How will you know?
   - How will the new teachers modify lessons for special needs students?

2. Discuss the following questions with the new teachers and ask how they will decide the answers to these questions.

   - What should students have a *REAL understanding* of that will last and carry over?
   - What should they be *familiar with* that can be built upon in later years?
   - What should they have an *awareness level* of that will be built upon in later years?
   - What should ELL learners be expected to know?
   - How do special education students' plans relate?

Formative and Summative Assessments

Formative Assessment Is Practice—The Dress Rehearsal

It is authentic, ongoing, sit beside, self-assessing, learn as we go, practice, group work, conversations, checklists, surveys, drill, practice tests.

When will new teachers use formative assessments in teaching?

Summative Assessment Is Final—The Opening Night of the Play

It is the final test, grade given to an individual student, final evaluation, judgment given at the end of the unit or term, report card grade, SAT final product, paper test, project artwork, final performance, Spanish oral exam.

When will new teachers use summative evaluation?

Using Rubrics and Portfolios to Assess Performance

Rubrics are either holistic or analytical. Holistic scoring values the student's overall thinking and understanding. The score is applied to the overall quality of the task completed. Analytical rubrics award points for each step the student completes in the process.

Review samples of rubrics with the new teachers.

1. Discuss specific criteria for a good paper, project, or performance.

2. Define degrees of understanding and demonstration.

   Examples:

   - Accuracy: Completely accurate, almost accurate, not accurate.
   - Clarity: Thoughts are clear, thoughts are hard to understand.
   - Understanding: Complete, almost, doesn't understand.

3. Discuss student portfolios. Share samples and ask new teachers to explain what they already know.

Progress Documentation and Record Keeping Strategies

Teachers use a variety of systems to keep track of student progress. A common way is to use a gradebook. However, many teachers use different systems within their gradebooks. Ask your cooperating teacher to share his or her system with you.

Share your teacher's gradebook system.

____

____

____

____

In addition to using gradebooks, you may make anecdotal comments and use journals, index file boxes, or make notes in your plan book to keep track. Other teachers use checklists or progress charts. Ask new teachers to find three other ways to record information and why a teacher might use these systems in addition to a gradebook.

____

____

____

____

How do you decide whether a record keeping system is effective? Ask new teachers to . . .

____ Review a strategy, ask—Is it easy to use? (Is it something I will use?)

____ Ask—Is it easy to read? (Can you scan it quickly for information?)

____ Ask—Can I derive patterns from it? (Over time do I see student progress?)

____ Use a highlighter to mark the holes in your gradebook to scan for missing grades easily.

____ Use another color highlighter for any grade below average to scan problem areas quickly.

Can Students Monitor Their Own Progress?

Discuss ways the new teachers can encourage their students to check for understanding. Using these question; as a guide, new teachers can include their students in the assessment process.

Hard or Easy?

- Ask students whether they are finding the work hard or easy.
- Make a graph to see how many students are finding things hard or easy.

What Are You Learning?

- Take a minute at the end of each class as part of your closing to ask students to write two things they learned in class today.
- Collect and review to see how you did as a teacher in presenting your objectives. This exercise can serve two purposes: (1) to see what they recall and (2) to let you know how to plan the next lesson.

More Time?

- Have students vote whether they think they need more time on a concept.
- Let students reply anonymously on paper or by putting their heads down and raising their hands.
- Write your own prediction of how the lesson went and what they will say before reading the students' responses.

Work Habits

Create a worksheet that asks questions that the students have to rate from 1 to 5. For example:

- I worked hard in groups today
- I understand the concepts presented.

Teacher Assessment

Create a sheet about you and your skills in teaching. Rate each 1 to 5. For example:

- My teacher presents information in a way I can understand.
- My teacher listens to my questions.
- There is time in class for me to practice the skill.

Communicating with Students about Their Progress

Teachers use a variety of systems to communicate with their students and keep them on track. The most common formats are the progress slip and the report card. Many teachers show these to students first, before they are sent home. Remember that progress may include growth in behavior as well as academics.

In addition to these traditional approaches, teachers are using other procedures to directly communicate with students. Discuss and share samples/ideas of any of the following communication systems you use.

1. *Student mailboxes/teacher mailbox.* Teachers and students can leave notes for one another about assignments, papers due, makeup work, for example.
2. *Student conference.* Teacher establishes a schedule and meets with individual students privately about progress. All students meet with teacher, not just failing students.
3. *Progress chart.* A subject-related progress chart is given to each student that visually documents the number of assignments completed, scores, projects, for example.
4. *Warnings.* When in danger of failing, a student receives a "red" note.
5. *Compliments.* Written or verbal acknowledgment of quality work.
6. *Checklist.* Placed inside daily or weekly folders—students can see what has been checked by you and approved for credit.
7. *Progress list.* Secondary students may be instructed to maintain their own grades.
8. *Midterm progress reports.* These list completed assignments and suggestions for improvement.
9. *Student-led parent conference.* When students attend and share their progress with the parents.
10. *Other ideas.*

Classroom and Behavior Management Issues

Ask your new teachers to list the three most common classroom misbehaviors they experience. Invite them to share how they are handling each issue. Discuss as a group how to avoid these disruptions to learning. Categorize the issues they bring up. Do they relate to routines, student issues, or lack of planning? How can the new teacher minimize these disruptions?

Misbehavior	How it is being handled	How to avoid it or minimize it
1.		
2.		
3.		

Ask new teachers to share what they learned from doing this process together.

Looking at Student Work

What are the new teachers' expectations for their students? Ask them to share what they expect their students to know and be able to do. How do these expectations relate to the district standards?

What are teachers looking for in assignments?

Ask each new teacher to bring several samples of ONE student's work to a meeting. The new teacher gives the papers to another new teacher or to you. What "story" can be told from looking at this student's work? Ask the new teacher to share his or her perspective about this student.

What does this work say about this student?	What is the evidence?	What is the next learning step for this student?

Discuss why it is important to use data and evidence to make decisions about students.

Communicating with Parents

Progress Reports and Report Cards

Discuss the school and district systems for reporting pupil progress. Are standard formats used? Are progress reports done on computer? Are report cards done on computer? Also discuss informal systems teachers may use for sharing progress with parents.

Formal Communication

Review the forms the new teachers need to complete to communicate progress to parents. Share your own personal tips for completing them easily. If a narrative is required on a report card, share samples of narratives you have written. Be sure to remind new teachers to check their spelling and grammar on all formal communication on progress reports or report cards. Partner up new teachers in your building so they can read each other's comments.

Informal Teacher Communication

- *Between Formal Progress Reports*

  Sometimes there is a need to contact parents between the formal cycle. Students who were failing may be doing well, and new teachers need to let the parents know that their support made a difference. Or parents may want to check in to see if the student is doing better because they may need to continue the monitoring at home. Share the formats you have used to communicate progress. Do you use a note? A checklist? Ask the new teachers how they would like to do it. They may have some new ideas about this.

- *Students Who Are Failing*

  If a student fails a test or a major project, it is usually a good idea to tell the parents. Some teachers send the test home and require a signature so the parents can see what was missed. If a meeting is required, then the parents know exactly what the meeting is about and the student could also be present.

- *The Notebook*

  Many teachers use a notebook that goes from home to school every day or once a week. This communication from parents to teacher keeps an open line of communication.

● REFLECT *on This Month's Discussions*

Mentor's Reflections

Directions: Complete as many of the bubble prompts as you would like after you have finished the Activites in the chapter and before you Set Goals. Add your own prompts to blank bubbles if these prompts do not meet your needs. Ask your new teacher(s) to complete their own reflection bubbles on the next page. Compare and share your reflections at one of your meetings. You may consider using one or two reflection bubbles as topics for future mentoring discussions.

Something I would like to show my new teachers in my classroom . . .
A recommendation I have right now is . . .
One way I can be helpful is . . .
I am excited about . . .

New Teachers' Reflections

Directions: Complete as many of the bubble prompts as you would like after you have finished the Activites in the chapter and before you Set Goals. Add your own prompts to blank bubbles if the prompts listed do not meet your needs. Compare and share your reflections with your mentor and other new teachers at a scheduled meeting.

Something that is really working is . . .

I continue to be challenged by . . .

I need help . . .

My class is . . .

• SET GOALS *for Next Month*

Directions:

- Complete this Set Goals page the last day of the month after your Reflection and use it to guide the first week meeting for next month.
- Review the PLAN–CONNECT–ACT pages you completed in this chapter to see what you need to revisit next month based on the new teachers' needs. List two needs that stand out for you right now.
- Ask yourself how you would like to share what the new teachers need with them.

  Will you give a tour of your classroom?

  Will you share materials you have made?

  Will you take them to the library and show them how to use existing resources?

  Will you connect them with people who can assist them regularly?

  What will you do to be an effective mentor?
- List two goals for yourself as a mentor for next month. How do your goals relate to what observe the new teachers' top two needs to be?

New Teacher Needs (from reflections, conversations, and your observations)	Your Mentor Goals
1.	1.
2.	2.

December

A good teacher is someone who listens to you as a student and always tries to challenge you —Fifth-Grade Student

Maintaining Balance

Teaching and Keeping the Students Interested

New Teacher Phase: Can I Do This?

"I'm having trouble keeping the students on task, and I am losing valuable teaching time."

INTASC Principles

Introduce the new teacher to INTASC Principle 4.

- **PRINCIPLE 4 Instructional Strategies/Problem Solving**
  The teacher understands and uses a variety of instructional strategies to encourage students' development of critical thinking, problem solving, and performance skills.

  Review previous discussions of Principles in September through November.

Maintaining Balance

Teaching and Keeping the Students Interested

Students know good teachers. Like the fifth-grade quote on the previous page says, "A good teacher is someone who listens to you as a student and always tries to challenge you." In this high technology world it is a challenge to keep students' attention. New teachers who don't know what students are capable of doing may give them work that is too easy. Students want to be challenged and want to succeed. Assist the new teachers in implementing a variety of strategies that will forward student learning. Remind them to listen to the students to find out what they like and how they learn best. Curriculum can be so overwhelming that many new teachers just want to "get it done" and move on, forgetting that students need to be at the center of any curriculum work.

As the new teachers question themselves and ask, "Can I do this?" you need to be prepared to demonstrate effective strategies and encourage them to continue to try new approaches. Maintaining their balance in December is important. Work with new teachers to find out what the "tipping point" is for each of them. See how you with the other new teachers can create a supportive environment to promote learning as well as to have some fun.

Use the pages this month to . . . Plan your monthly meetings by deciding what you would like to talk about as well as to set meeting dates for the month, think about how you will Connect your new teachers to available resources, select Activities that make sense for you to discuss, Reflect at the end of the month, and Set Goals for next month. Use all of these process pages as a guide to enrich the quality of your monthly mentoring conversations.

What Do We Want to Talk about When We Meet This Month?

Invite your new teachers to write down a short list of questions and bring them to your first December meeting. Use the questions below as a guide for your discussions throughout the month.

New Teachers' Possible Questions:

1. Can you help me select a variety of strategies that will work for me?
2. I need help incorporating problem solving into my lessons. What should I do?
3. Critical thinking is important, but I have to cover so much content. How can I incorporate that skill into my lessons?
4. What are the successful strategies you have used that encourage students to think?
5. I am losing track of the other INTASC principles we covered from September to November. There is so much to know. Can you review them with me?

List the other questions your new teachers brought to the meeting so you will have them for your next mentoring cycle.

As a Mentor, You Can Ask Questions, Too!

Try to ask more questions to learn about your new teachers, rather than telling them how things should be done.

Mentor's Possible Questions:

1. What is working for you right now in your classroom?
2. When are your students most interested in learning?
3. What do you most enjoy about teaching and why do you think that is so?
4. What can I do to assist you right now that would reduce your anxiety?

● PLAN *Agendas and Schedule Meetings*

Plan your monthly meetings, decide when and how you want to Connect with each other as well as others in the school and community, select the Activities from this chapter that make sense for you to discuss, Reflect separately at the end of the end of the month and share your reflection, and Set Goals for next month.

PLAN *Agendas for Monthly Meetings Based on New Teacher Needs*

Planning quality conversations means that the needs of the new teacher must be met. Take time to complete the chart before making decisions about what you will discuss at your monthly mentoring sessions. What makes most sense for you as a mentor to share in December?

Complete this together and save for future discussion. Make a copy for each new teacher if needed.

What is needed and wanted in December?

New Teacher *I need . . .*	Mentor *I want to share . . .*

When Will We Meet?

Plan to meet at times that allow you to have quality time together without interruptions. Knowing when you will meet reduces anxiety for both of you all month. New teachers look forward to planned meetings.

When will you meet?

How many times during the month?

How long will you meet for quality conversations? Ten, twenty, or thirty minutes? Indicate that on this calendar.

Will your new teacher observe you teach and demonstrate a skill this month?

Will you observe the new teachers this month? Purpose of the observation is . . .

Are there other teachers or community members your new teachers need to connect with this month? Indicate on this schedule.

Make a copy of this calendar for each new teacher. Also put these times into your teaching plan book.

December Calendar

MONDAY	TUESDAY	WEDNESDAY	THURSDAY	FRIDAY

Key: B = before school D = during the day (preparation time or lunch time) A = After school

● CONNECT *with People, Readings, Professional Associations, Resources, and Technology*

What resources exist in your school and community that could assist new teachers in maintaining balance?

Directions:

1. Review the answers you both completed in the "What is needed and wanted?" boxes on page 118. What does the new teacher need? What do you want to share? Keep the answers to these questions in mind when you explore possible resources.
2. Copy this Connect page so you both can investigate resources separately. Bring your completed December Plan "What is needed and wanted?" and Connect pages to the next meeting and compare what you both discovered. If you are working with a group of new teachers, make copies of all of their completed Connect pages and distribute the resource ideas to everyone in the group.

CONNECT *with People . . .*

Who in the school building (experienced teachers, other beginning teachers, custodians, secretaries, etc.) may be able to help with December needs?

What agencies in the community relate to the topics, instructional strategies, and problem solving?

How can parents be helpful this month?

CONNECT *with Readings, Professional Associations, and Resources . . .*

What have you read or used that would assist in using a variety of instructional strategies to develop critical thinking, problem solving, and performance skills? New teachers may refer to student teaching courses and readings. Mentors may have books that relate to this topic.

CONNECT *with Technology . . .*

Find websites and links that will provide information about:

- Instructional strategies for your grade level
- Problem-solving ideas for teachers
- Critical thinking
- Teaching for understanding
- Making content meaningful at ______ grade level

● ACTIVITIES: *Select Topics for Quality Discussions*

What Will We Discuss at Our December Meetings?

Each month begins with a formal first week planning meeting where dates and times for discussions are scheduled. Use the agenda in this chapter to guide your meeting. Select Activity pages listed on this page as possible talking points at this meeting or for any other meetings you schedule during the month. Record your meeting dates and time on your Planning calendar. You may decide to assign some Activity pages to the new teacher for completion alone. Use the Appendix for five-, ten-, fifteen-, twenty-, thirty-, and sixty-minute meeting formats you may want to use during the month.

Schedule this meeting during the first week of the month	**PLAN the Monthly Discussions (see sample agenda)**
✓ The Activities you will discuss	**ACT by Selecting Appropriate Topics for Discussions during the Month**
	Activities for December discussions related to *Students* include . . .
	ACT 1 Revisiting Behavior Management
	ACT 2 Keeping Special Needs Students Engaged in Learning
	ACT 3 Avoiding Common Problems and Keeping Students Interested
	ACT 4 When Is It Time to Seek Additional Support?
	ACT 5 Problem Solving and Critical Thinking
	* ACT 6 Classroom and Behavior Management Issues
	* ACT 7 Looking at Student Work
	* ACT 8 Communicating with Parents
The last day of the month the new teachers and you complete these pages on your own.	**REFLECT and SET GOALS for Next Month** **Give new teachers copies of REFLECT and SET GOALS pages to bring to the January first week meeting.**

*These three Activities will be offered each month.

First Week Agenda: Making a Plan for the Month

TOPIC: Maintaining Balance: Teaching and Keeping Students Interested

Have snacks and water or soft drinks available. Hold the meeting in your classroom or another comfortable space where you will be sure you will not be interrupted. Put a colorful sign on your door that says "Mentoring Meeting—Please do not disturb."

First: Welcome and introductions: Invite the new teachers to share something that is going well.

Then: Review the November new teacher Reflections.

- How did the new teachers respond? How will this impact what you do next?
- Share any of your mentor Reflections that are appropriate.

Next: Review the Set Goals page that you both completed the last day of November.

- How will these goals carry over into this month?
- What do we want to talk about when we meet this month?
- Share the possible key questions listed at the beginning of this chapter.
- What most interests the new teachers right now?

Begin: Plan what you will discuss this month use the Planning calendar to set your meeting times. Think about how you should share information with the new teachers. Will you give handouts, a tour of your room, or hold discussions? Review the Activities pages for handouts and discussion ideas. Use the Appendix for five-, ten-, fifteen-, twenty-, thirty-, and sixty-minute meeting templates. Modify Activities and templates as needed.

Network: Complete the Connections page together.

Acknowledge: Recognize what you and the new teachers have done so far instead of focusing on what they don't know. Remind the new teachers that they will complete Reflections and Set Goals pages on their own the last day of the month to bring to the first week meeting the next month.

Share: End the session with compliments for each new teacher and at least one practical idea related to keeping students engaged. Let new teachers share ideas with each other, too.

Revisiting Behavior Management

At this point in the year, your new teachers may be having some difficulty. They certainly will be tired, and they might need to review the basics. Take some time to go back to August orientation ideas as well as to provide new ways to have them deal with any disruptive behaviors that may be occurring in the classroom.

Invite the new teachers to take a deep breath and to review their own discipline and behavior management philosophy. Ask them to think about the way they may be responding to inappropriate behavior and why they might be responding that way.

What is your discipline philosophy? How does it compare to the new teachers'? Describe an incident that has occurred and show how it could be handled two different ways depending on the teacher's philosophy.

Incident: ____

One way to respond:

____

____

____

____

Another way to respond:

____

____

____

____

Discuss positive appropriate ways to deal with recurring misbehavior.

Keeping Special Needs Students Engaged in Learning

New teachers need to continually think about ways in which they can modify lessons for the diverse learners in their classrooms. By December these continual modifications get tiring, and sometimes new teachers just want to keep moving. Take some time to review individual education plans (IEPs) with the new teachers who have students with special needs in their classrooms because these plans often have examples of modifications that should be used. These often simple approaches can be used with other students in the classroom as well.

Examples of modifications:

- ☐ Giving a student more time to complete an assignment.
- ☐ Assigning fewer questions or examples to be completed.
- ☐ Allowing students to tape-record their answers instead of writing.
- ☐ Working with a partner who would write the answers the student stated verbally.
- ☐ Accepting printed work instead of cursive.
- ☐ Using the computer to complete work.

Think about these questions:

How do you know which activities you can leave incomplete and which have to be done?

How do you pace a lesson so that all or most students complete the task?

How do you create high expectations for learners who work more slowly?

Discuss with new teachers how lessons are currently being modified for individual students in their classrooms. List the student and the modification in the lesson plans.

Student 1 ____________________ Modification ____________________

Student 2 ____________________ Modification ____________________

Student 3 ____________________ Modification ____________________

Student 4 ____________________ Modification ____________________

Student 5 ____________________ Modification ____________________

Avoiding Common Problems and Keeping Students Interested

Review these key areas that could lead to discipline problems.

- *Classroom Management.* Have you structured your classroom in an orderly way to avoid potential problems? Traffic flow? Room setup? What could you change to avoid any further issues?
- *Lesson Planning.* Have you designed lessons that meet the needs of all students so they don't get frustrated and angry? Are the lessons challenging but doable? Do you have accommodations for grouping that avoid discipline issues? How can you redesign lessons to avoid future discipline problems you are experiencing?
- *Discipline—Rules, Rewards, and Consequences.* Are the rules clearly posted and understood? Do students "own" them or are they imposed on them? Are you consistent when you apply the consequences? Do you treat all students fairly? What do you need to do to be sure your rules, rewards, and consequences are working to avoid problems?

Keep Track of What Is Working!

It is so easy to stay focused on the one student who is gaining all the attention in your classroom. You certainly want everyone to behave and listen to you. Don't forget, you are doing many things right! List the behaviors you are observing in your classroom that are positive and list why you think they are working. What are you doing to maintain that behavior? Keep it up!

Classroom Behavior	What You Are Doing	Why Is It Working?
Class is passing in papers in an orderly way every day with their names on them!	Stopping class three minutes before the bell to allow time to pass in papers.	Consistently ask students to check their names and pass in papers.

When Is It Time to Seek Additional Support?

Explain to the new teachers that sometimes students need more help than they can provide. It is not their fault when students come to school with issues that are beyond repair in a classroom setting. Some students need medical and psychological help, and a new teacher needs to know when to get it. As a mentor, you will be able to consult with the new teacher to get the appropriate assistance for the student.

How do you know when you need more help?

____ When you have exhausted your possibilities.

____ When the student exhibits serious problems beyond the scope of common issues.

____ When your mentor has determined the student needs additional help.

____ When parents have indicated a need for support.

What should new teachers do?

____ Maintain accurate records of all misbehaviors with dates of offenses.

____ Write a request for help with your mentor.

How do new teachers know they haven't failed?

____ They have tried a number of approaches with the student and documented them.

____ Their mentor teacher has advised the student needs additional help.

Problem Solving and Critical Thinking

Discuss the strategies you have used to enhance students' problem-solving abilities. If you are a secondary teacher, how do these strategies relate to your content? Solving problems engages learners. Invite the new teachers to share the problem-solving strategies they are using.

Critical thinking allows students to go beyond the basic memorization and to actually engage with the content. Find several examples of critical thinking in your own teaching and share them with the new teachers. Why is this so important?

Performance skills are natural ways for students to share what they know and are able to do. Students enjoy plays, reading poetry, writing original stories, drawing, and dancing. Discuss ways in which these important skills can be integrated into daily lessons and units.

List examples here:

Sports are also ways in which students may use problem solving.

Discuss how problem solving, critical thinking, participation in sports, and performance skills can reduce behavior problems.

Classroom and Behavior Management Issues

Classroom and School Problems

Discuss recurring problems new teachers are having with individual students or the whole class. Review the four categories below and assist the new teachers in identifying the issues. Are these solutions appropriate options? Add your own ideas to the discussion.

Problems	What You Need to Do
Chronic Work Avoidance Evidenced, for example, by being absent regularly, fooling around in class, not passing in assignments, tardiness.	• Make sure student is capable of work. • Keep accurate records of what is missing. • Talk with mentor teacher. • Let student know how assignments affect grade. • Talk with parents. • Other?
Habitual Rule Breaking Evidenced, for example, by calling out in class, not bringing pencil to class regularly, being talkative, forgetting other materials.	• Use consequences established. • Try behavior modification systems. • Talk with student privately. • Discuss issue with mentor teacher. • Talk with parents. • Other?
Hostile Verbal Outbursts Evidenced, for example, by angry loud yelling, chip-on-the-shoulder attitude, defiance when asked to complete assignments.	• Determine whether the outburst is just momentary. • Don't engage in a power struggle. • Remove the student if anger persists. • Talk with mentor teacher. • Talk with principal. • Talk with guidance counselor. • Talk with parents. • Other?
Fighting, Destruction, Weapons, Alcohol or Drug Abuse Evidenced, for example, by hallway pushing, violence with peers, threats, glazed look in class.	• Send a student for help. • Disperse crowds that may gather to watch. • Calmly talk; do not shout or scream. • Report the incident immediately. • Other?

Looking at Student Work

Using Criteria to Assess Performance

Discuss the indicators of success for student work. How does a teacher know students have learned? How does a teacher use data to analyze student work? Designing rubrics and making lists of indicators of success allow teachers to use concrete evidence to demonstrate progress. What indicators or criteria are used in your district?

Randomly select a sample of student work from a completed set of papers and discuss how you know it fits into one of these categories.

Below Standard	Meets the Standard	Above Standard
What indicates that it is below standard? Be specific in your discussion.	What evidence shows this work meets the standard? Check the indicators.	What makes you say it is above the standard? Be specific.

Now look at the whole set of completed papers from the whole class. Sort the papers into these categories.

Below Standard	Meets the Standard	Above Standard
How many papers here? % of class _____	How many papers here? % of class _____	How many papers here? % of class _____

Why is this discussion important to have with your new teachers?

Communicating with Parents

One sure way to keep students interested in school is to compliment them for what they are doing right! Parents and students love to hear good news. Because the school day is so hectic and the needs of failing students have to be a priority for a new teacher, there often is not time to compliment the students who are doing well. Discuss the ways new teachers can systematically let students and parents know students are progressing. Two ideas here will get your discussion started.

Compliment Phone Calls

Invite the new teachers to bring a class list to a meeting. If they completed the Student Profile in September, they could bring that, too. The idea is that every student in the class will get a compliment for something in December. New teachers can think of it as a holiday gift to the student and the parents. The new teacher makes a few phone calls each night and leaves a message on an answering machine or speaks personally to the parents. More than one compliment call can be made in a night. No one gets two calls until everyone in the class is called once.

> The message script is . . . This is an official *Compliment Phone Call* from Mr. Jones, Susan's teacher at Sunnyside School. I am calling to compliment your daughter for her outstanding work in class this week. She worked with other students who needed help, she answered questions in class, and she did very well on her project. Please let Susan know that she received this compliment. Have a great day!

The new teachers should not get into long conversations with parents at this time. This is not a conference, it is a compliment for something very specific. This is BRIEF, so it can fit into the new teacher's day.

Positive Notes

This compliment could be given electronically as an email or e-card, or it could be a Compliment Postcard from the teacher. The key is to be specific about what is being complimented so the student is clear about what positive behavior or academic performance is. The goal for the new teachers is to identify good behavior and reward it by telling the parents.

The goal is to compliment every student in the class in December. Some will be more challenging than others, but every student is doing something right. The new teachers just need to find it with your help. The next morning in class after their first compliment calls, new teachers will notice students' responses.

Notes for New Teachers

Keep track of any ideas you may have during the week, for the end of the calendar year, or for the new year here.

December

● REFLECT *on This Month's Discussions*

Mentor's Reflections

Directions: Complete as many of the bubble prompts as you would like after you have finished the ACTivites in the chapter and before you SET GOALS. Add your own prompts to blank bubbles if these prompts do not meet your needs. Ask your new teacher(s) to complete their own reflection bubbles on the next page. Compare and share your reflections at one of your meetings. You may consider using one or two reflection bubbles as topics for future mentoring discussions.

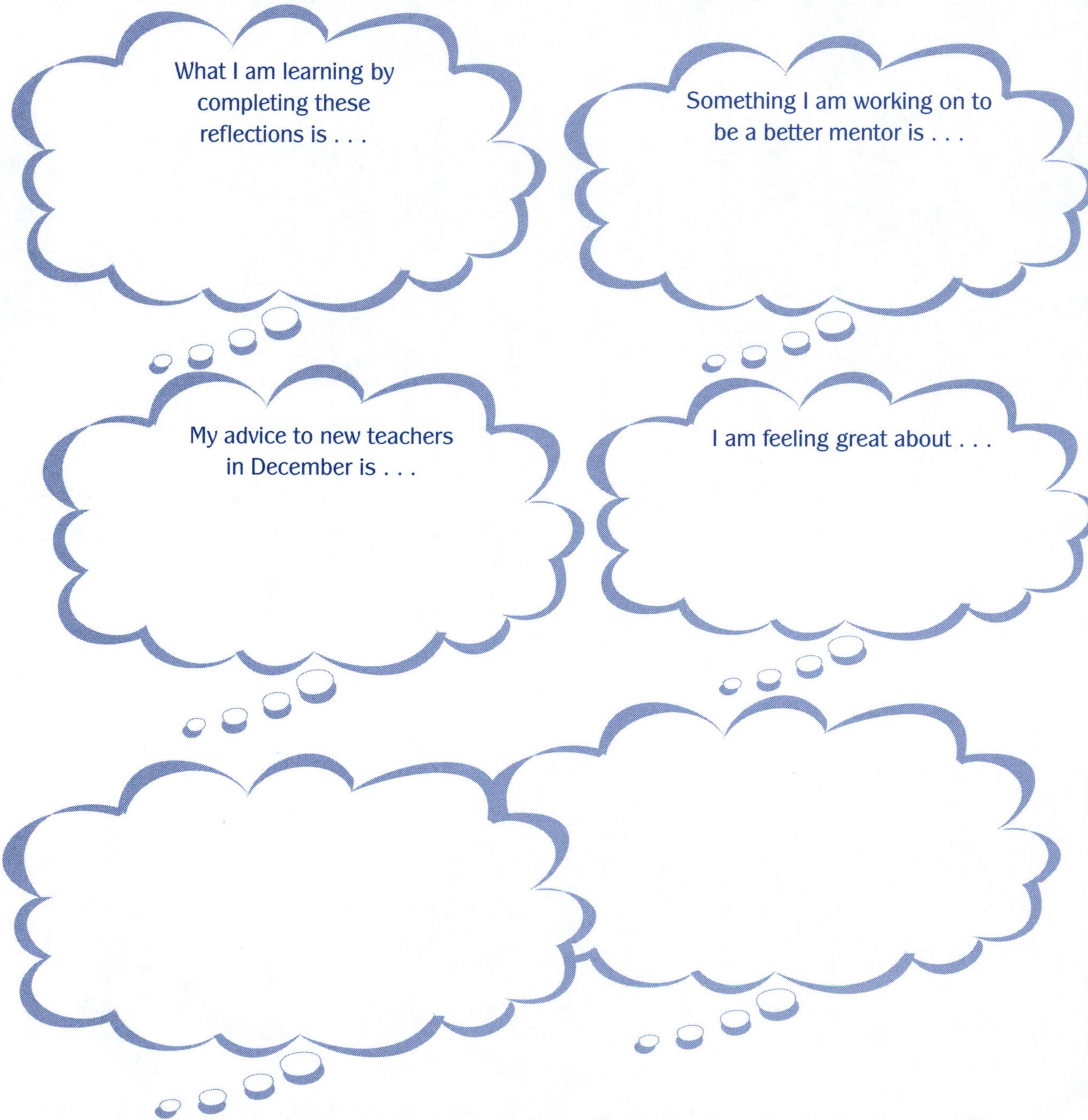

What I am learning by completing these reflections is . . .
Something I am working on to be a better mentor is . . .
My advice to new teachers in December is . . .
I am feeling great about . . .

New Teachers' Reflections

Directions: Complete as many of the bubble prompts as you would like after you have finished the Activites in the chapter and before you Set Goals. Add your own prompts to blank bubbles if the prompts listed do not meet your needs. Compare and share your reflections with your mentor and other new teachers at a scheduled meeting.

I am frustrated by . . .

I need to . . .

I really love . . .

The best way to describe this year so far is . . .

● SET GOALS *for Next Month*

Directions:

- Complete this Set Goals page the last day of the month after your Reflection and use it to guide the first week meeting for next month.
- Review the PLAN–CONNECT–ACT pages you completed in this chapter to see what you need to revisit next month based on the new teachers' needs. List two needs that stand out for you right now.
- Ask yourself how you would like to share what the new teachers need with them.

  Will you give a tour of your classroom?

  Will you share materials you have made?

  Will you take them to the library and show them how to use existing resources?

  Will you connect them with people who can assist them regularly?

  What will you do to be an effective mentor?
- List two goals for yourself as a mentor for next month. How do your goals relate to what observe the new teachers' top two needs to be?

New Teacher Needs **(from reflections, conversations, and your observations)**	**Your Mentor Goals**
1.	1.
2.	2.

I think patience makes a good teacher. —Second-Grade Student

Beginning a New Calendar Year

Looking Back and Moving Forward

New Teacher Phase: Refreshed and Ready

"I want to start the year over again because I know so much more now."

INTASC Principles

Introduce the new teacher to INTASC Principle 9.

- **PRINCIPLE 9 Professional Growth/Reflection**
  The teacher is a reflective practitioner who continually evaluates the effects of his or her choices and actions on others (students, parents, and other professionals in the learning community) and who actively seeks out opportunities to grow professionally.

Beginning a New Calendar Year

Looking Back and Moving Forward

Patience does make a good teacher, just like the second-grade student says in the quote on the previous page. Allow the new teachers with whom you are working to be patient with themselves. They don't have to learn everything in the first year of teaching. They are growing and developing with each new experience and interaction with their students. Sometimes they are moving so quickly they don't even see what they are learning. Be patient with the new teachers and ask them to be patient with themselves and their students. The beginning of a new calendar year is a perfect opportunity to look back to what you did in August and to look ahead to what you plan for June. Be the guide they need to see the light at the end of the year. Be the patience they need right now.

The holiday vacation may bring the new teachers back refreshed and ready to begin. Others may be more cautious and concerned that they can't do this work. Be with the new teachers wherever they find themselves. Use this month to ground them in reflective practice and goal setting. New Year's resolutions are fun to make and easy to break. Design doable measurable goals with the new teachers. Encourage them to see what is working as well as what isn't. This month's INTASC standard is about professional growth and decision making. Discuss the ways teachers make decisions and how these impact student learning.

This month two new topics are being added to the Activities list: Observing New Teachers and Preparing a Professional Portfolio. You may, in fact, never have an opportunity to observe the new teacher in the classroom this year, so the pages from January through June offer suggestions for ways the new teacher can self-reflect and discuss ideas with you. A Professional Portfolio may be required in your district or state. If it is, the January–June pages will keep you and the new teachers on track for completing it. Use all of these process pages as a guide to enrich the quality of your monthly mentoring conversations.

What Do We Want to Talk about When We Meet This Month?

Invite your new teachers to write down a short list of questions and bring them to your first January meeting. Use the questions below as a guide for your discussions throughout the month.

New Teachers' Possible Questions:

1. I would like to share ideas and learn from others. How do I connect with other new teachers?
2. What opportunities are available in the district, through the teachers' union, or from local professional development providers?
3. In your professional opinion, what should I focus on to improve my practice for the rest of the year?
4. Is there a way I could easily connect with the parents and the community that would assist me in my teaching?
5. Do you have any suggestions for assisting me in reflecting more systematically so I don't lose my good ideas?

List the other questions your new teachers brought to the meeting so you will have them for your next mentoring cycle.

As a Mentor, You Can Ask Questions, Too!

Try to ask more questions to learn about your new teachers, rather than telling them how things should be done.

Mentor's Possible Questions:

1. Do you keep a journal? Why or why not? How do you reflect on your practice?
2. Are you a member of a professional organization?
3. What changes have you already made in what you are doing and why?
4. What can I do to assist you right now that would reduce your anxiety?

● PLAN *Agendas and Schedule Meetings*

Plan your monthly meetings, decide when and how you want to Connect with each other as well as others in the school and community, select the Activities from this chapter that make sense for you to discuss, Reflect separately at the end of the end of the month and share your reflection, and Set Goals for next month.

PLAN *Agendas for Monthly Meetings Based on New Teacher Needs*

Planning quality conversations means that the needs of the new teacher must be met. Take time to complete the chart before making decisions about what you will discuss at your monthly mentoring sessions. What makes most sense for you as a mentor to share in January?

Complete this together and save for future discussion. Make a copy for each new teacher if needed.

What is needed and wanted in January?

New Teacher *I need . . .*	Mentor *I want to share . . .*

When Will We Meet?

Plan to meet at times that allow you to have quality time together without interruptions. Knowing when you will meet reduces anxiety for both of you all month. New teachers look forward to planned meetings.

When will you meet?

How many times during the month?

How long will you meet for quality conversations? Ten, twenty, or thirty minutes? Indicate that on this calendar.

Will your new teacher observe you teach and demonstrate a skill this month?

Will you observe the new teachers this month? Purpose of the observation is . . .

Are there other teachers or community members your new teachers need to connect with this month? Indicate on this schedule.

Make a copy of this calendar for each new teacher. Also put these times into your teaching plan book.

January Calendar

MONDAY	TUESDAY	WEDNESDAY	THURSDAY	FRIDAY

Key: B = before school D = during the day (preparation time or lunch time) A = After school

● CONNECT *with People, Readings, Professional Associations, Resources, and Technology*

What resources exist in your school and community that could assist new teachers in looking back and moving forward?

Directions:

1. Review the answers you both completed in the "What is needed and wanted?" boxes on page 138. What does the new teacher need? What do you want to share? Keep the answers to these questions in mind when you explore possible resources.
2. Copy this Connect page so you both can investigate resources separately. Bring your completed January Plan "What is needed and wanted?" and Connect pages to the next meeting and compare what you both discovered. If you are working with a group of new teachers, make copies of all of their completed Connect pages and distribute the resource ideas to everyone in the group.

CONNECT *with People . . .*

Who in the school building (experienced teachers, other beginning teachers, custodians, secretaries, etc.) may be able to help with January needs?

Who in the professional community or district inspires professional growth and reflection?

How could parents be helpful in reflecting on the past few months and looking forward?

CONNECT *with Readings, Professional Associations, and Resources . . .*

What have you read or used that assist in reflection and goal setting for the new calendar year? New teachers may refer to student teaching courses and readings. Mentors may have books that relate to this topic.

CONNECT *with Technology . . .*

Find websites and links that will provide information about:

- Teacher reflection
- Goal setting for the second half of the year
- Reflective practice
- Writing about practice
- Professional development

● ACTIVITIES: *Select Topics for Quality Discussions*

What Will We Discuss at Our January Meetings?

Each month begins with a formal first week planning meeting where dates and times for discussions are scheduled. Use the agenda in this chapter to guide your meeting. Select Activity pages listed on this page as possible talking points at this meeting or for any other meetings you schedule during the month. Record your meeting dates and time on your Planning calendar. You may decide to assign some Activity pages to the new teacher for completion alone. Use the Appendix for five-, ten-, fifteen-, twenty-, thirty-, and sixty-minute meeting formats you may want to use during the month.

Schedule this meeting during the first week of the month	**PLAN the Monthly Discussions (see sample agenda)**
✓ The Activities you will discuss	**ACT by Selecting Appropriate Topics for Discussions during the Month**
	Activities for January discussions related to *Moving Forward* include . . .
	ACT 1 Looking Back
	ACT 2 Moving Forward
	ACT 3 What Do I Believe?
	ACT 4 Constructing a Sociogram
	ACT 5 Using Drawings to Gain Student Perspective
	ACT 6 Social Activities and a Sense of Humor!
	* ACT 7 Classroom and Behavior Management Issues
	* ACT 8 Looking at Student Work
	* ACT 9 Communicating with Parents
	* ACT 10 Observing New Teachers
	* ACT 11 Preparing a Professional Portfolio
The last day of the month the new teachers and you complete these pages on your own.	**REFLECT and SET GOALS for Next Month** **Give new teachers copies of REFLECT and SET GOALS pages to bring to the February first week meeting.**

*These five Activities will be offered each month from January through June.

January

● *First Week Agenda: Making a Plan for the Month*

TOPIC: Beginning a New Calendar Year: Looking Back and Moving Forward

Have snacks and water or soft drinks available. Hold the meeting in your classroom or another comfortable space where you will be sure you will not be interrupted. Put a colorful sign on your door that says "Mentoring Meeting—Please do not disturb."

FIRST: Welcome and introductions: Invite new teachers to share something that is going well.

Then: Review the December new teacher Reflections.

- How did the new teachers respond? How will this impact what you do next?
- Share any of your mentor Reflections that are appropriate.

Next: Review the Set Goals page that you both completed the last day of December.

- How will these goals carry over into this month?
- What do we want to talk about when we meet this month?
- Share the possible key questions listed at the beginning of this chapter.
- What most interests the new teachers right now?

Begin: Plan what you will discuss this month use the Planning calendar to set your meeting times. Think about how you should share information with the new teachers. Will you give handouts, a tour of your room, or hold discussions? Review the Activities pages for handouts and discussion ideas. Use the Appendix for five-, ten-, fifteen-, twenty-, thirty-, and sixty-minute meeting templates. Modify Activities and templates as needed.

Network: Complete the Connections page together.

Acknowledge: Recognize what you and the new teachers have done so far instead of focusing on what they don't know. Remind the new teachers that they will complete Reflections and Set Goals pages on their own the last day of the month to bring to the first week meeting the next month.

Share: End the session with compliments for each new teacher and at least one practical idea related to beginning a new year. Let new teachers share ideas with each other, too.

Looking Back

Discuss the successes and challenges of the first part of the year with the new teachers. Let them share them in their own words. Some new teachers are harder on themselves because they are disillusioned with their impact on students.

Invite the new teachers to write letters to themselves acknowledging their successes and noting the challenges they still face. Do this writing at a meeting where they have some privacy and some time to think about what has happened. Purchase stationery with colorful borders and colorful pens. The new teachers can select paper and pens that fit their mood. Give them the following instructions:

Directions: Write a letter to yourself that highlights areas of growth, new insights about teaching and learning, or successes. Also include one challenge you are facing that you would like to discuss with your mentor. Finally, share what you would like to be acknowledged for so far this year. Share your letter with your mentor and other new teachers. Celebrate your growth and set goals for the rest of the year.

Note: If the challenge the teacher identifies relates to one student in the classroom, you may want to use this process as well.

Directions: Write a journal entry from the perspective of the most difficult student in the classroom. The new teacher needs to imagine that the class has been given the assignment to write about their own lives and something that is going on for them. The teacher has also indicated that the students can write about school and how they are doing right now.

This is a very powerful process and is especially enlightening when a small group of new teachers share their entries with each other. As a mentor facilitator, assist the new teachers in discovering the issues that may be impacting that student and how the new teacher may respond to make this situation less disruptive.

Moving Forward

Review the letters the new teachers wrote and celebrate their successes. Set goals with each new teacher to attack challenges in systematic ways. New teachers often take their struggles personally, and it worries them that they can't do something well or can't make one student be respectful. Use your skills as a mentor to dissect the problem and make it manageable and measurable. Remind the new teachers that all problems cannot be solved. There are some things teachers cannot change about students' lives. Assisting new teachers in strategies for letting go of issues they can't do anything about is important at this time of year.

What Are New Teachers Worried About?
Problems to Possibilities

1. Ask the new teachers to write their most challenging problems or worries on *blue* sticky notes (symbolizes what makes the new teacher "blue"). Ask the new teachers to work together to classify the problems into categories—e.g., student misbehavior, managing paperwork, organizing the room, parent issues—and write that on the top of the sticky note. Invite new teachers to share the problems with each other. Adapt categories as needed to make common categories understood by all new teachers. New teachers may complete as many "worries" as they want.

2. Place the problems on the Worry Wall at the front of the room in categories as defined by the classifications at the top of the sticky notes.

3. Invite new teachers to walk up to the wall and read all the problems and think about the possible solutions to any of them. Using *yellow* sticky notes, the new teachers can place possible solutions on any problems. They can provide multiple solutions to as many problems as they want.

4. The new teachers who originally placed the problems on the wall now go back and pick them up with the solutions attached to them. Let new teachers talk in pairs about what they received for possibilities.

Discuss categories and types of solutions with the entire group at the end of the meeting. Your goal as a mentor is to always provide possible solutions to existing issues and to use available resources (like other new teachers) to do that. Reminding new teachers that they can't be all things to all students is important.

What Do I Believe?

At this time of year it is important for new teachers to revisit the philosophy statements they may have written in college or for their job applications. Explain why it is important to revisit their beliefs and ideas about teaching and learning periodically. As a mentor, you should do this too! What do you believe about mentoring? What is your mentoring philosophy? Use this exercise to revisit your ideas and share them with other mentors or your mentor coordinator.

Directions: Dictate the following questions to the new teachers. Ask them to think about, What do I believe about teaching and learning right now? How do I see myself?

First, list three words that describe you as a teacher.

1. ____________________
2. ____________________
3. ____________________

Then list three words your students would use to describe you as a teacher.

1. ____________________
2. ____________________
3. ____________________

How do these compare? Why are they alike or different? Share.

Now think about your beliefs about teaching and learning. Complete this prompt twice.

I believe . . .

I also believe . . .

Finally, list one way you are demonstrating what you believe in the classroom. What are you doing that shows what you believe or who you are (as described in your descriptive words)? Set Goals with new teachers so they can actualize their qualities and beliefs related to their philosophy of education in the classroom. How can you do more of this? Share.

Constructing a Sociogram

Assist your new teachers in constructing a sociogram to gather information about what the students believe enhances their learning. One way to illustrate the dynamics in a classroom is to construct a sociogram. You can use the information to design cooperative groups or teams. Have them draw the relationships out on a piece of paper after they collect the data so they can see who the stars and isolates are in the classroom. It will also let you know what the students think of each other and where you may have to step in to include some students that you may not have realized were excluded. Discuss why this is important information for a new teacher to know.

Step 1 Ask students in the classroom to list three students, by first, second, and third choice, whom they would prefer to work with in the classroom. (Make a distinction between work partners and social partners outside of school.) Tell them it is for possible future group projects and that you may use it to try and create teams with at least one person they prefer to work with.

Step 2 Have the students write why they selected each student. This will give you some insight, and themes may repeat themselves.

Step 3 Collect the data and make a grid with students' names across the top and down the left side. Graph paper works well. Place a 1, 2, or 3 under the student's name as indicated to show choices.

Example

	Kas	*Carlos*	*Germaine*	*Olga*
Kas	—	1	3	2
Carlos	3	—	1	2
Germaine	3	2	—	1
Olga	3	2	1	—

Step 4 Tally choices to indicate most preferred working partners (commonly called *stars*) and least selected working partners (referred to as *isolates*).

Using Drawings to Gain Student Perspective

Drawing or doodling can provide information to teachers for any grade level from preschool through high school. Drawing allows students to use images to express themselves. Color, shapes, and abstract designs all can give the new teacher some insight into what the students think about learning in this room with this teacher. The key to this type of assessment is to have the new teacher be clear about the question.

The new teacher could give the assignment herself—or to get more honest results—she could invite another new teacher or you to give the directions to one of the prompts she has selected from the list below.

You should also try this process by having the new teacher ask your students to complete one of the drawing prompts. What would you want to know about your teaching from your students' perspectives?

Here are some basic prompts. Feel free to create one of your own!

Draw a picture of your teacher (leave it very general—see what students do).

Draw a picture of your teacher in the classroom (again, leave it general—just in the classroom).

Draw of picture of your teacher teaching (keep it general).

Draw a picture of the classroom (don't mention the teacher).

Draw a picture of yourself (the student) in the classroom (this would give some insight as to what the student thinks).

Draw a picture of yourself (the student) learning something in the classroom.

Obviously, the directions for younger students may have to be more explicit. Some teachers might say, if a camera was brought into this room, what would it see? Draw a . . . just like the camera would.

Explain to the students why the assignment is being given. Talk with new teachers to decide what to say to students in regard to this.

Discuss drawings and how they were helpful for understanding students.

Social Activities and a Sense of Humor!

Most of your meetings are probably spent trying to resolve issues, share challenges, and discuss problems. Even though there is a place for acknowledgment, it often gets buried by pressing emotional worries the new teachers bring to the table. Make this activity just about FUN. Take some time to talk about things that new teachers might enjoy doing socially. Do they want to have a school social? A reception? A party? A movie night? This would just be for them, not the students, not the parents, not the mentors with them—just new teachers. Assist them in finding space, resources, and the time to do this. New teachers need to connect with each other and find some time to laugh abut what is happening in their classrooms. Perhaps they will want to schedule something in every month. Encourage your new teachers to take time for themselves! Here are some ideas to consider.

New Teacher Appreciation Day (or night or Saturday)

The mentors may want to organize a social event for the new teachers, too. Perhaps go to a play or a show together, or just out to dinner. Maybe the school could even pay! This should be social, fun, and welcoming.

Social Life Survival Directory

New teachers that move in from other states or towns may not know where to go for great meals or social interaction. They have been so busy teaching they probably have not done many things and many complain they have "no social life." Create a Social Survival Directory for the new teachers. Have fun doing it!

Sense of Humor Booklet

Invite the new teachers to share how they use their sense of humor in the classroom with students. Create a list of humorous situations they have encountered and share them Laugh! Have fun!

Remind the new teachers that talking about students, their parents, or any other school issue is not appropriate at any event. Everyone has had an experience where you have heard gossip and inappropriate information being transferred about students. Professionalism and confidentiality must be a priority for new teachers. Have fun but not at others' expense.

Classroom and Behavior Management Issues

Typical Situations for Teachers: What Would You Do If . . .

Use the cases on this page to brainstorm possible solutions with the new teachers. Make the case fit the grade level you are working with. Expand the details to illustrate what the student would do at that grade level. For example, a sleeping student (Case 6) may be handled very differently in an early childhood classroom as opposed to a high school English class. List three possible solutions for each case and let new teachers try them in their own classes. Discuss what happens at your next meeting.

- *Case 1:* The Class Clown

  The class clown comes in late and tells jokes every day during class. Everyone loves her and laughs so hard it is difficult to get their attention. Valuable class time is being wasted.

- *Case 2:* The Bully

  This girl hits at least one person a day. She walks by people and punches their arms, or she trips anyone who walks by her desk. She is the terror of the playground.

- *Case 3:* The Lie

  A very likable student who always completed his homework lied and said he had handed it in one day. The teacher discovered he had not done it at all and just called out YES when she asked students during roll call.

- *Case 4:* A Destructive Student

  A very quiet student exhibits aggressive behavior by quietly breaking pencils at his desk while the teacher is giving the directions.

- *Case 5:* Shouting Out

  This student is so excited and wants to participate in class discussions. She always shouts out the answers when the new teacher asks the class general questions. No one else has a chance to even talk.

- *Case 6:* Sleeper

  This student slumps over his desk in the back of the room. He is not disturbing anyone but he is not learning the material either. He is in danger of failing the class.

- *Case 7:* Cheating

  This student was caught cheating on a test. The answers were clearly on her hand and she was copying them onto her paper. She had cheated before and at that time said she would not do it again.

- *Case 8:* A Fist Fight

  Two students hit each other in the hallway outside the teacher's door about a personal issue.

Looking at Student Work

Identify Patterns

Ask new teachers to bring a whole set of completed papers to a meeting. Sort the papers into these categories or into the categories in the rubric, if a different one is provided.

Below Standard	Meets the Standard	Above Standard
How many papers here? % of class _____	How many papers here? % of class _____	How many papers here? % of class _____

1. Look at all the papers in the Below Standard category or the lowest category in your rubric.

   What is the pattern?

   Are the students making similar mistakes?

   What could the new teacher do next to move these students to Meets the Standard?

2. Look at all the papers in the Meets the Standard category.

   What is the pattern?

   Are the students making similar mistakes?

   What could the new teacher do next to move these students to Above Standard?

Communicating with Parents

Parent Meetings to Set Goals for the New Year

New teachers will feel a bit more revitalized after a break from school, and you can assist them in setting new goals for communicating with parents. Encourage your new teachers to set up meetings with the parents of students they are finding particularly challenging.

Sample Meeting Agenda

1. *Opening the Meeting*

   I am so glad you could join me today in discussing John's progress.

   The purpose of this meeting is . . .

   Can you tell me some things that are going on at home or outside of school right now . . .

   You know your child better than I do, can you give me some insights so I can help him be successful in school?

2. *Sharing the Positive*

   This is what I see going well for John right now . . .

   This sample of work shows he can . . .

   I also know that John is very good at . . .

3. *Standards and Curriculum Goals*

   These are the learning goals for ___ grade this year.

   Let's look at the areas where John needs assistance . . .

   By the end of the year John needs to meet _______ standards

   My concerns for John are . . .

4. *Working Together to Set Goals*

   How can we assist John together?

   One thing you could do at home is . . .

   When should we meet again to check on John's progress?

Observing New Teachers

Self-Observation: Reflecting on Practice

The most powerful observation for new teachers is looking at themselves. When new teachers take time to reflect on their own practice, they begin to see what they are doing well and how to modify their instruction and interaction. Invite each new teacher you are working with to select one lesson to evaluate in depth. Each should bring his or her lesson plan and a copy of the responses to the questions below to a meeting to discuss what each can learn from self-reflection.

1. Did the students learn from my lesson? Were they actively engaged? How do I know?
2. How closely did I follow my lesson plan? Did I have to modify during the lesson? Why?
3. What do I think was the most effective part of the lesson?
4. Were the materials/visuals/aids appropriate? Why? Why not?
5. What would I change/keep the same the next time I do this lesson?
6. What do I see as my teaching strengths?

Preparing a Professional Portfolio

Some districts require new teachers to prepare a portfolio as part of their induction responsibilities for the state requirements for certification. If the new teachers do not have to do this as part of the licensing requirement, you may still want to assist them in collecting a variety of materials they can use to document their year in the classroom. Portfolios are very useful visual displays of actual work and demonstration of competency and professional growth. Encourage the new teachers to collect many of the items listed below. No need to organize them yet. Every month there will be a Preparing a Professional Portfolio activity to move you along in the process.

Inventory of Possible Artifacts for Portfolio

____ Diagram of classroom, i.e., floor plan, photos, or both

____ Lesson plans created by new teacher

____ Unit plans interrelating subject areas, including the arts, thematic, and others.

____ Cooperative learning techniques

____ Classroom management and discipline strategies

____ Samples of student work: each subject area, advanced work, work adapted for diverse needs, homework, tests, artwork, performance assessment

____ Audiotapes of students in groups; you introducing a lesson

____ Videotapes (permission slip) of students during a lesson; documentary of classroom

____ Materials from pre-practicum that may be highlighted

____ Materials from methods course

____ Photographs of classroom, bulletin boards, group lessons (permission slips from students)

____ Documentation of any honors or awards

____ Appreciation letters, notes from parents, notes from students

____ Evaluations from others, mentor teacher recommendation, supervisor evaluation

____ Professional profile (third-person bio page) to go with résumé

____ Books and articles read with how they helped you to be a better teacher

____ Inspirational writings, poems, or artwork that might serve as titles for pages or cover

____ Other?

● REFLECT *on This Month's Discussions*

Mentor's Reflections

Directions: Reread all the Reflections you completed from August through December. Then complete all of the bubble prompts below. Share your responses with your mentor coordinator or other supportive administrator to improve the program.

Ask your new teachers to complete their own reflection bubbles on the next page and to bring them to your next meeting. Combine all the responses and anonymously share them with your mentor coordinator or supportive administrator so the new teachers' voices will be heard.

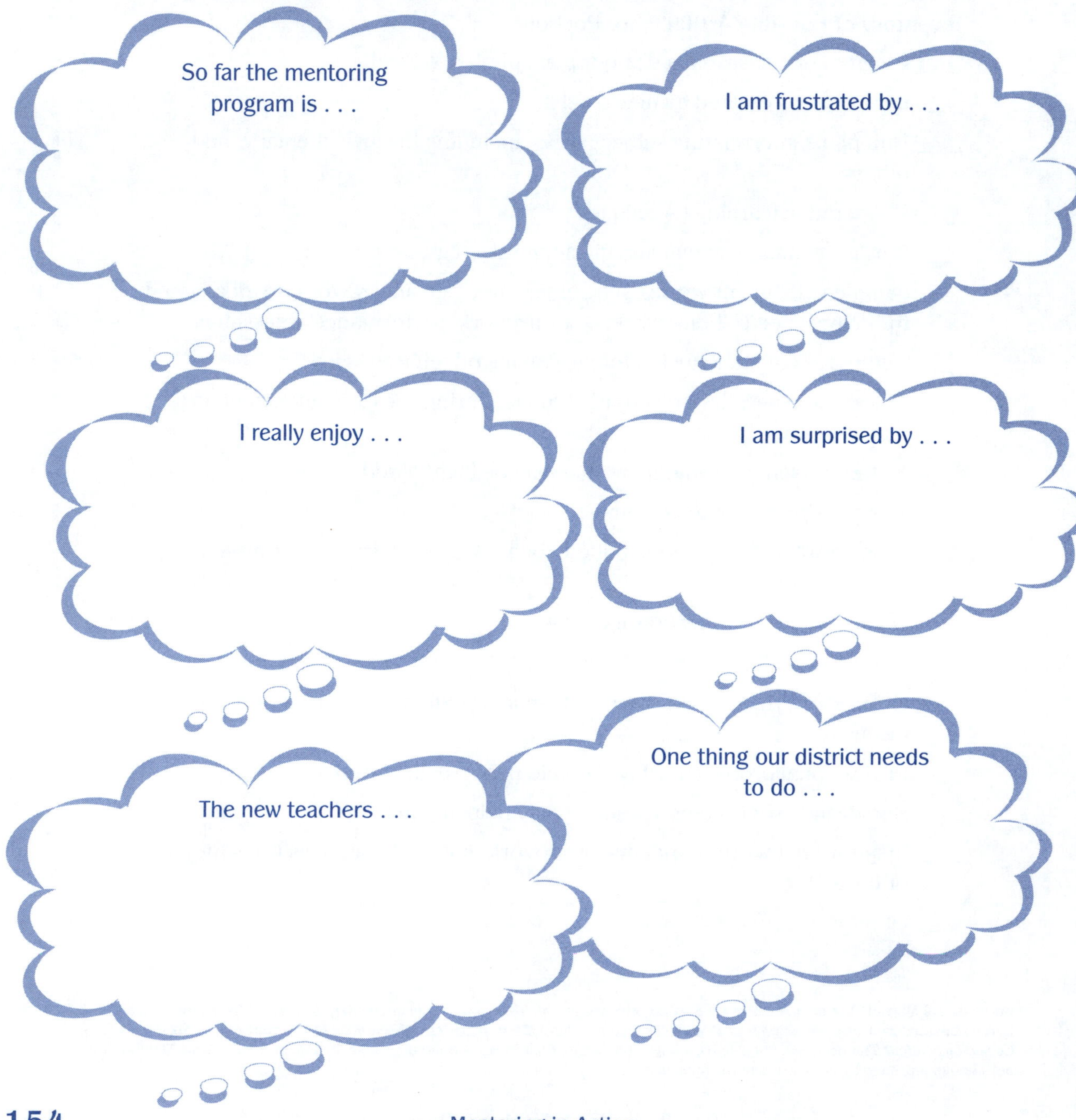

So far the mentoring program is . . .
I am frustrated by . . .
I really enjoy . . .
I am surprised by . . .
The new teachers . . .
One thing our district needs to do . . .

New Teachers' Reflections

Directions: Reread all the Reflections you completed from August through December. Then complete all of the bubble prompts below. Share your responses with your mentor and other new teachers as your next scheduled meeting. All the responses from all new teachers will be combined and anonymously shared with the mentor coordinator so your voices will be heard.

What I like about the mentor program is . . .

My mentor has helped me . . .

One thing that would make a difference for the rest of the year is . . .

I am really pleased with . . .

I wish the district could . . .

I wish my mentor could . . .

● SET GOALS *for Next Month*

Directions:

- Complete this Set Goals page the last day of the month after your Reflection and use it to guide the First Week meeting for next month.
- Review the PLAN–CONNECT–ACT pages you completed in this chapter to see what you need to revisit next month based on the new teachers' needs. List two needs that stand out for you right now.
- Ask yourself how you would like to share what the new teachers need with them.

  Will you give a tour of your classroom?

  Will you share materials you have made?

  Will you take them to the library and show them how to use existing resources?

  Will you connect them with people who can assist them regularly?

  What will you do to be an effective mentor?
- List two goals for yourself as a mentor for next month. How do your goals relate to what observe the new teachers' top two needs to be?

New Teacher Needs (from reflections, conversations, and your observations)	Your Mentor Goals
1.	1.
2.	2.

What I think makes a good teacher is that they can teach all kinds of things your parents don't know. –Sixth-Grade Student

Engaging Students in the Curriculum

Focus on Content through Active Inquiry

New Teacher Phase: Staying Focused

"There is so much to teach before the end of the school year. How will I do it all?"

INTASC Principles

Introduce the new teacher to INTASC Principle 6.

- **PRINCIPLE 6 Communication/Knowledge**
  The teacher uses knowledge of effective verbal, nonverbal, and media communication techniques to foster active inquiry, collaboration, and supportive interaction in the classroom.

Engaging Students in the Curriculum

Focus on Content through Active Inquiry

At this time of year it is important to just keep the new teachers focused on what they are doing. There is so much to do that new teachers sometimes get so scattered that they don't know what to do first. Break the curriculum down into bite-sized pieces that the new teachers can understand and implement. The curriculum usually is the most challenging part of the first year for new teachers because they are teaching it for the first time. Remember when you taught a new unit for the first time. This is how the new teachers feel every day, every period of the day!

This chapter highlights the continued use of varied teaching strategies as well as the opportunity to give students choices in the classroom. When a teacher can give options to students about what they can do for homework, for example, the students have to engage in the conversation and commit to something. It is more likely they will actually do their homework if they selected it! Ultimately, it may not matter which homework assignment is completed or how or if the content is learned. Assist the new teachers in developing these strategies.

INTASC Principle 6 (Communication/Knowledge) will focus the discussion on the ways in which the new teachers use effective verbal, nonverbal, and media communication techniques to foster active inquiry in their classrooms. Make time to share these valuable strategies. What do you do to engage students in your classroom?

Use the pages this month to . . . Plan your monthly meetings by deciding what you would like to talk about as well as to set meeting dates for the month, think about how you will Connect your new teachers to available resources, select Activities that make sense for you to discuss, Reflect at the end of the month, and Set Goals for next month. Use all of these process pages as a guide to enrich the quality of your monthly mentoring conversations.

What Do We Want to Talk about When We Meet This Month?

Invite your new teachers to write down a short list of questions and bring them to your first February meeting. Use the questions below as a guide for your discussions throughout the month.

New Teachers' Possible Questions:

1. How do I get my students to support each other and work together?
2. Are there easy ways to integrate media and audiovisual aids into my lessons?
3. I want to foster active inquiry in my lessons, but it just gets too complicated. Can you suggest some teachers I could observe who use this technique to engage their students?
4. I feel like I am talking too much. What are some nonverbal ways I could communicate with my students that will create a supportive environment for learning?

List the other questions your new teachers brought to the meeting so you will have them for your next mentoring cycle.

As a Mentor, You Can Ask Questions, Too!

Try to ask more questions to learn about your new teachers, rather than telling them how things should be done.

Mentor's Possible Questions:

1. What are your goals for creating a collaborative learning environment?
2. How do you communicate these goals to your students?
3. What would you do if you could do anything in your classroom right now?
4. What can I do to assist you right now that would reduce your anxiety?

PLAN *Agendas and Schedule Meetings*

Plan your monthly meetings, decide when and how you want to Connect with each other as well as others in the school and community, select the ACTivities from this chapter that make sense for you to discuss, Reflect separately at the end of the end of the month and share your reflections, and Set Goals for next month.

PLAN *Agendas for Monthly Meetings Based on New Teacher Needs*

Planning quality conversations means that the needs of the new teacher must be met. Take time to complete the chart before making decisions about what you will discuss at your monthly mentoring sessions. What makes most sense for you as a mentor to share in February?

Complete this together and save for future discussion. Make a copy for each new teacher if needed.

What is needed and wanted in February?

New Teacher *I need . . .*	Mentor *I want to share . . .*

When Will We Meet?

Plan to meet at times that allow you to have quality time together without interruptions. Knowing when you will meet reduces anxiety for both of you all month. New teachers look forward to planned meetings.

When will you meet?

How many times during the month?

How long will you meet for quality conversations? Ten, twenty, or thirty minutes? Indicate that on this calendar.

Will your new teacher observe you teach and demonstrate a skill this month?

Will you observe the new teachers this month? Purpose of the observation is . . .

Are there other teachers or community members your new teacher(s) need to connect with this month? Indicate on this schedule.

Make a copy of this calendar for each new teacher. Also put these times into your teaching plan book.

February Calendar

MONDAY	TUESDAY	WEDNESDAY	THURSDAY	FRIDAY

Key: B = before school D = during the day (preparation time or lunch time) A = After school

● CONNECT *with People, Readings, Professional Associations, Resources, and Technology*

What resources exist in your school and community that could assist new teachers in engaging students in the curriculum?

Directions:

1. Review the answers you both completed in the "What is needed and wanted?" boxes on page 160. What does the new teacher need? What do you want to share? Keep the answers to these questions in mind when you explore possible resources.
2. Copy this Connect page so you both can investigate resources separately. Bring your completed February "What is needed and wanted?" and Connect pages to the next meeting and compare what you both discovered. If you are working with a group of new teachers, make copies of all of their completed Connect pages and distribute the resource ideas to everyone in the group.

CONNECT *with People . . .*

Who in the school building (experienced teachers, other beginning teachers, custodians, secretaries, etc.) may be able to help with February needs?

Who in the professional community could assist with ideas for communication techniques?

How can parents be used as resources for communication and media techniques?

CONNECT *with Readings, Professional Associations, and Resources . . .*

What have you read or used that would assist increasing your knowledge of verbal, nonverbal, and media communication techniques to foster active inquiry, collaboration, and supportive interaction in the classroom? New teachers may refer to student teaching courses and readings. Mentors may have books that relate to this topic.

CONNECT *with Technology . . .*

Find websites and links that will provide information about:

- Collaboration in the classroom
- Inquiry as a technique for active learning
- The use of media in the classroom

● ACTIVITIES: *Select Topics for Quality Discussions*

What Will We Discuss at Our February Meetings?

Each month begins with a formal first week planning meeting where dates and times for discussions are scheduled. Use the agenda in this chapter to guide your meeting. Select Activity pages listed on this page as possible talking points at this meeting or for any other meetings you schedule during the month. Record your meeting dates and time on your Planning calendar. You may decide to assign some Activity pages to the new teacher for completion alone. Use the Appendix for five-, ten-, fifteen-, twenty-, thirty-, and sixty-minute meeting formats you may want to use during the month.

Schedule this meeting during the first week of the month	**PLAN the Monthly Discussions (see sample agenda)**
✓ The Activities you will discuss	**ACT by Selecting Appropriate Topics for Discussions during the Month**
	Activities for February discussions related to *Content Knowledge* include . . .
	ACT 1 Using Varied Teaching Strategies
	ACT 2 Giving Students Choices to Enhance Learning
	ACT 3 Homework and Opportunities for Enrichment
	ACT 4 How Much Time?
	* ACT 5 Classroom and Behavior Management Issues
	* ACT 6 Looking at Student Work
	* ACT 7 Communicating with Parents
	* ACT 8 Observing New Teachers
	* ACT 9 Preparing a Professional Portfolio
The last day of the month the new teachers and you complete these pages on your own.	**REFLECT and SET GOALS for Next Month** **Give new teachers copies of REFLECT and SET GOALS pages to bring to the March first week meeting.**

*These five Activities will be offered each month from January through June.

February

First Week Agenda: Making a Plan for the Month

TOPIC: Engaging Students in the Curriculum: Focus on Content Through Active Inquiry

Have snacks and water or soft drinks available. Hold the meeting in your classroom or another comfortable space where you will be sure you will not be interrupted. Put a colorful sign on your door that says "Mentoring Meeting—Please do not disturb."

First: Welcome and introductions: Invite new teachers to share something that is going well.

Then: Review the January new teacher Reflections.

- How did the new teachers respond? How will this impact what you do next?
- Share any of your mentor Reflections that are appropriate.

Next: Review the Set Goals page that you both completed the last day of January.

- How will these goals carry over into this month?
- What do we want to talk about when we meet this month?
- Share the possible key questions listed at the beginning of this chapter.
- What most interests the new teachers right now?

Begin: Plan what you will discuss this month use the Planning calendar to set your meeting times. Think about how you should share information with the new teachers. Will you give handouts, a tour of your room, or hold discussions? Review the Activities pages for handouts and discussion ideas. Use the Appendix for five-, ten-, fifteen-, twenty-, thirty-, and sixty-minute meeting templates. Modify Activities and templates as needed.

Network: Complete the Connections page together.

Acknowledge: Recognize what you and the new teachers have done so far instead of focusing on what they don't know. Remind the new teacher(s) that they will complete Reflections and Set Goals pages on their own the last day of the month to bring to the first week meeting the next month.

Share: End the session with compliments for each new teacher and at least one practical idea related to engaging students with content. Let new teachers share ideas, too.

Using Varied Teaching Strategies

Encourage your new teachers to assess the ways they are delivering information to students in the classroom.

- *Use both auditory and visual directions.* Students in the classroom may be auditory or visual learners. Giving directions in both written and oral forms will include these varied learners. Also, be aware of giving multiple directions, especially orally, that students of varied levels may not be able to retain. Write directions on the board or overhead projector and leave them up throughout an activity so they can be referred to at any time.
- *Demonstrate concepts by using visual examples.* After directions are given and the student teacher feels students understand, specific examples should be given to concretely show what is expected. This does not mean students are supposed to copy the example. It is to provide a visual prop that is used by the teacher to demonstrate what is expected.
- *Allow for choice when appropriate.* If possible, provide several activities that meet the same objective and allow students to choose the one with which they feel most comfortable. Example: If the goal is to solve a word problem in math, choices for solving could include paper and pencil, manipulatives, working alone, or working with a partner. The point is that you want the students to use their best learning style to solve the problem.
- *Plan for varied paces.* Students think and work at different speeds. The faster thinkers are not necessarily the most accurate or the most creative problem solvers. Don't be trapped by rewarding only the quickest students, because you may be missing some outstanding problem solving. Sometimes it is appropriate to leave a task incomplete. Doing a portion of some math problems can show you whether the students understand the concept.
- *Assist students who need support.* Some students will need additional support during a lesson because they do not understand the directions or are unable to complete the task. You may not have time to walk around the room and meet with these students individually. One strategy is to let them work with a partner who is able to explain more clearly what is expected. These "partner coaches" can be selected before class begins, and they do not have to have their own work done to assist.

Giving Students Choices to Enhance Learning

Allow for student choice whenever possible. Students usually know how they learn best, and if you can offer them a variety of ways in which to show you that they know the material, they will feel more successful and will be more invested in the work.

Examples of ways choice can be incorporated into your classroom:

- Choosing a homework assignment from three that are acceptable.
- Choosing a partner to work with on a project.
- Choosing an independent reading book.
- Choosing the type of test (multiple choice, essay, short answer).
- Creating a test by choosing all the items that would go on the test.

List other ways to incorporate choice into your classroom that would promote student interest.

____

____

____

Example of how choice of strategy could be used to meet an objective:

To solve a particular work problem, students could choose to

- Use paper and pencil.
- Use manipulatives.
- Draw the answer.
- Work alone.
- Work with a partner.
- Act out the answer.

Can you think of ways in which you could provide your students with choice without disrupting curriculum and while supporting the needs of diverse learners?

____

____

____

Homework and Opportunities for Enrichment

Enrichment

Enrichment can be offered to students who have a deeper interest in the topic or those who may complete classwork early (and accurately). Special activities in a learning center, questions on the board, or enrichment sheets provide opportunities for more connection to a particular topic.

Discuss enrichment activities for gifted and talented students, students who complete work early, or students who have a genuine interest in this topic.

Ideas for enrichment:

____

____

Note: Enrichment should not just be a reward for those who complete their work early. Students who have varying paces may never have a chance to try more challenging activities offered. Create one day a month as "enrichment" period and let students select a topic they truly enjoy learning about. These topics could become "clubs" where students meet regularly to learn more about what they like.

Homework

Discuss homework policies. Do students have to pass in homework? Is it always required? Does it only relate to the text? Do students get to select homework activities? Is homework extra credit? Does your mentor teacher correct homework? If not, how does it count toward the grade? Is there such a thing as "creative" homework?

What happens if students don't do their homework? For example, students are assigned a chapter to read in a book and you designed a lesson around the expectation that they had read it. What do you do about the planned lesson?

How Much Time?

Work with the new teachers to find out how much time they spend on different parts of their lesson. Do they spend enough time trying to engage the learners with the content? Are they using active inquiry to engage learners?

Sample

Topic	*Time Starts*	*Time Ends*	*Total*
Introduction to lesson	__________	__________	__________
Giving directions	__________	__________	__________
Lecturing	__________	__________	__________
Answering questions	__________	__________	__________
Asking questions	__________	__________	__________
Practice work	__________	__________	__________
Reprimanding	__________	__________	__________
Checking for understanding	__________	__________	__________
Students actively engaged/ demonstrating learning	__________	__________	__________

What took up the most time during the lesson?

____

____

____

What took up the least time during the lesson?

____

____

____

Share this information with the new teacher and ask how the time spent relates to the original plan.

Classroom and Behavior Management Issues

Reward your students for good behavior. The key to rewards is finding out what students really value. Each grade level is very different. Ask the new teachers to share what they think would be valuable to the students in their classes. Then encourage them to ask their students and then compare the ideas.

Here are some typical rewards for elementary and secondary students. What would you add? What would you never use? Why?

Elementary Rewards	*Secondary Rewards*
Free time	Free time
Watch a video	Read a magazine
Do errands for the teacher	Work on computer
Lead the line	See a film/video
Go to the reading center	Food
Pick out a book	Class trip
Play with the pet in class	Play sports during day
Listen to music in class	Listen to CD in class
Stickers	Wear a hat in class
Pencils	Use the video camera
Ice cream	Time off from school
A certificate	Be coach's assistant
Pizza party	Make a T-shirt
Magic markers	Teach a class
Free recess	Free homework pass
Sit next to a friend for a day	Read a newspaper

Looking at Student Work

What Should the Student Learn Next?

Ask new teachers to bring samples of student work that is below standard. It is often overwhelming to a new teacher to have a student or students who have so much to learn. Assist the new teachers in finding *one* skill that would be the next thing this student should learn. Taking underperforming learners and moving them step by step toward standards allow the student and the new teacher to feel some level of success. It also allows both of them to focus on one skill and identify it clearly. What should the student learn next that is developmentally appropriate?

Student	List several skills student is not meeting.	What *one* skill the student could focus on next to improve learning?
#1		
#2		
#3		
#4		

Discuss any patterns or trends that emerge in the new teachers' discussion about what one thing these students need to do next to learn.

Communicating with Parents

Monthly Content Updates

Discuss simple ways new teachers can share what content they are teaching in their classrooms. Parents need to know what the students are learning so when new teachers contact them they understand how they can be helpful at home. Parents can also be valuable resources to teaching. Use the update as a way to get volunteers or donations as well. One idea is to have new teachers send home a weekly notice listing what content is being taught.

Elementary teachers may use something like this. Secondary teachers would modify for one specific subject, such as English.

Content Update for February
Ms. Smith Grade 5

Content Areas	What We Are Learning	How You Can Help Us Learn . . .
Math	Fractions	Donate some manipulates we can use Come to class as a volunteer to tutor students
Science	Ecology unit (saving our rivers)	Be a guest speaker Allow us to visit you at your work, i.e., field trip
Social Studies	World War II	Be a guest speaker (you know about the war or a grandparent may have served in the war)
Language Arts	Writing letters	Sharing your letter writing skills and sample letters you have written Donating stationery, stamps, pens so the class can write real letters to people in a nursing home

Contact Ms. Smith at 552-XXXX if you can help our class this month. Thank you!

Discuss other ways new teachers can let the parents know what they are doing.

Observing New Teachers

New teachers can learn a lot by listening to themselves on tape. Assist the new teachers in getting audio equipment and tapes. Have the new teachers listen for the level of vocabulary they use during the lesson, their tone, how often they used their voice to reprimand or praise (and what that sounded like), how clear they were, and if they had to repeat themselves. What did their voice sound like to them? Was it high or low? Were they speaking too quickly? Was their voice engaging for learners?

1. List two or three things you would like to listen for in the audiotape and write them down.

   Examples: my tone of voice, whether I call on all girls or boys, how I respond to student questions, how I give directions.

   ____

   ____

   ____

2. Listen to the tape.

   What did you hear related to the areas listed in question 1?

   ____

   ____

   ____

   Ask yourself, "If I was a student in this class, would I be engaged in learning?"

   ____

   ____

   ____

   Sometimes you will hear unexpected surprises on the tape.

Preparing a Professional Portfolio

Encourage the new teachers to collect samples of their work all year. They can use a three-ring binder or box to begin the process. Then, toward the end of the year, the new teachers may want to display their artifacts in a professional portfolio with captions and brief descriptions. For now they should just think about collecting:

- Samples of student work with their comments
- Pages from this book related to reflection and goal setting
- Photographs
- Video and audio tapes
- Excerpts from their journal
- Sample lesson plans and units
- Comments from the mentor
- School activities (meetings, events, etc.)
- Professional growth (reading, memberships, writing, etc.)
- Successful classroom management and behavior management systems
- Other ideas?

Encourage the new teachers to share ideas at a meeting and discuss artifacts they think would be meaningful for their portfolios. If the teachers are participating in an Induction course for credit, they may need to include meeting times of classes or other requirements.

● REFLECT *on This Month's Discussions*

Mentor's Reflections

Directions: Complete as many of the bubble prompts as you would like after you have finished the Activities in the chapter and before you Set Goals. Add your own prompts to blank bubbles if these prompts do not meet your needs. Ask your new teachers to complete their own reflection bubbles on the next page. Compare and share your reflections at one of your meetings. You may consider using one or two reflection bubbles as topics for future mentoring discussions.

It is difficult to . . .
I like . . .
My reason for mentoring is . . .
A compliment I have for my new teachers . . .

New Teachers' Reflections

Directions: Complete as many of the bubble prompts as you would like after you have finished the Activities in the chapter and before you Set Goals. Add your own prompts to blank bubbles if the prompts listed do not meet your needs. Compare and share your reflections with your mentor and other new teachers at a scheduled meeting.

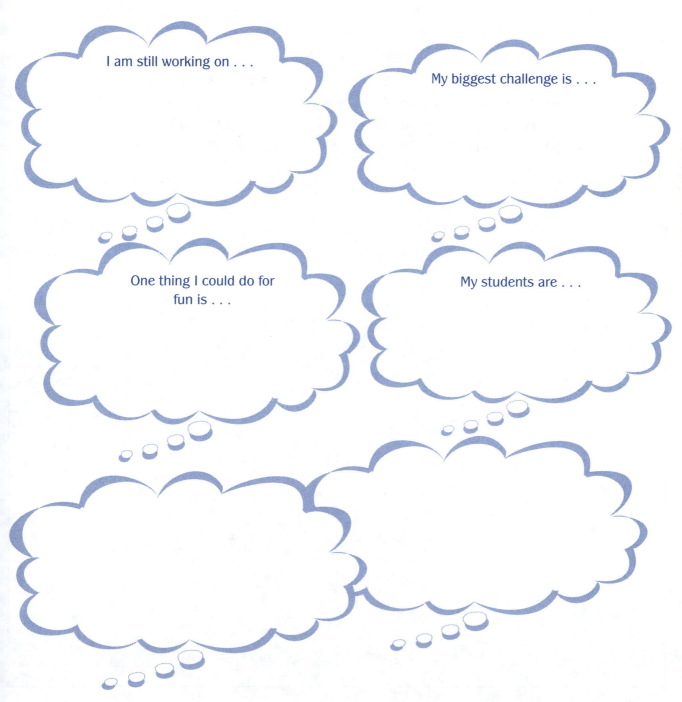

I am still working on . . .

My biggest challenge is . . .

One thing I could do for fun is . . .

My students are . . .

• SET GOALS *for Next Month*

Directions:

- Complete this Set Goals page the last day of the month after your Reflection and use it to guide the first week meeting for next month.
- Review the PLAN–CONNECT–ACT pages you completed in this chapter to see what you need to revisit next month based on the new teachers' needs. List two needs that stand out for you right now.
- Ask yourself how you would like to share what the new teachers need with them.

  Will you give a tour of your classroom?

  Will you share materials you have made?

  Will you take them to the library and show them how to use existing resources?

  Will you connect them with people who can assist them regularly?

  What will you do to be an effective mentor?
- List two goals for yourself as a mentor for next month. How do your goals relate to what observe the new teachers' top two needs to be?

New Teacher Needs (from reflections, conversations, and your observations)	Your Mentor Goals
1.	1.
2.	2.

March

In my opinion a good teacher is someone who teaches you what you need to know for everyday life and has fun doing it. –Eighth-Grade Student

Collaborating with New Teachers

Observing and Building a Trusting Relationship

New Teacher Phase: Collegiality

"I want to improve my practice. Can you help me?"

INTASC Principles

Introduce the new teacher to INTASC Principle 10.

- **PRINCIPLE 10 Interpersonal Relationships**
  The teacher fosters relationships with school colleagues, parents, and agencies in the larger community to support students' learning and well being.

Collaborating with New Teachers

Observing and Building a Trusting Relationship

Collaboration can be fun. Teaching has often been called an isolating profession, and many people think it is still that way. Today there are more opportunities to team teach, create curriculum together, work across disciplines, and create teacher study groups. Collaboration is work. It means meetings, discussions, and decisions based on input from more than one person. Some teachers think it just isn't worth it. Others have made it enjoyable and a refreshing part of a day spent mostly with students. Discuss collegiality and professionalism with the new teachers with whom you work. What does it mean to them? They may not have any idea!

The quote from the student on the previous pages lets you know that students notice when teachers are having fun doing what they are doing. It makes a difference if a teacher presents a lesson that he or she really likes. What do you like to teach? How do the students know you like it? As a mentor, share what you love about teaching and what is fun for you. Who are your collaborators at the school? Encourage the new teachers to be colleagues and to collaborate with each other.

INTASC Principle 10 (Interpersonal Relationships) highlights the importance of building relationships beyond the school. Think of ways in which your new teachers can connect with agencies, parents, and the business community. How will these professional relationships help their students learn?

Be sure to discuss or share the recurring issues pages with the new teachers. There will always be classroom and behavior management issues—you don't need to focus on this topic at every meeting. You may want to make copies of these Activities pages and put them in the new teachers' mailboxes to review in between meetings.

Use the pages this month to . . . Plan your monthly meetings by deciding what you would like to talk about as well as to set meeting dates for the month, think about how you will Connect your new teachers to available resources, select Activities that make sense for you to discuss, Reflect at the end of the month, and Set Goals for next month. Use all of these process pages as a guide to enrich the quality of your monthly mentoring conversations.

What Do We Want to Talk about When We Meet This Month?

Invite your new teachers to write down a short list of questions and bring them to your first March meeting. Use the questions below as a guide for your discussions throughout the month.

New Teachers' Possible Questions:

1. How can I get to know the other teachers in this school?
2. What are some of the local agencies I should be aware of that can assist me with students or that offer resources for teachers?
3. I would like to sponsor some kind of parent event in my classroom. Can you help me navigate school politics to do that?
4. What else do I need to know about relationships in this school that will assist me with my students?

List the other questions your new teachers brought to the meeting so you will have them for your next mentoring cycle.

As a Mentor, You Can Ask Questions, Too!

Try to ask more questions to learn about your new teachers, rather than telling them how things should be done.

Mentor's Possible Questions:

1. How can I help you connect with other new teachers in the school or district?
2. How are you getting along with other teachers right now?
3. What is your next step to connecting with parents?
4. What can I do to assist you right now that would reduce your anxiety?

PLAN *Agendas and Schedule Meetings*

Plan your monthly meetings, decide when and how you want to Connect with each other as well as others in the school and community, select the Activities from this chapter that make sense for you to discuss, Reflect separately at the end of the end of the month and share your reflection, and Set Goals for next month.

PLAN *Agendas for Monthly Meetings Based on New Teacher Needs*

Planning quality conversations means that the needs of the new teacher must be met. Take time to complete the chart before making decisions about what you will discuss at your monthly mentoring sessions. What makes most sense for you as a mentor to share in March?

Complete this together and save for future discussion. Make a copy for each new teacher if needed.

What is needed and wanted in March?

New Teacher *I need . . .*	Mentor *I want to share . . .*

When Will We Meet?

Plan to meet at times that allow you to have quality time together without interruptions. Knowing when you will meet reduces anxiety for both of you all month. New teachers look forward to planned meetings.

When will you meet?

How many times during the month?

How long will you meet for quality conversations? Ten, twenty, or thirty minutes? Indicate that on this calendar.

Will your new teacher observe you teach and demonstrate a skill this month?

Will you observe the new teachers this month? Purpose of the observation is . . .

Are there other teachers or community members your new teacher(s) need to connect with this month? Indicate on this schedule.

Make a copy of this calendar for each new teacher. Also put these times into your teaching plan book.

March Calendar

MONDAY	TUESDAY	WEDNESDAY	THURSDAY	FRIDAY

Key: B = before school D = during the day (preparation time or lunch time) A = After school

CONNECT *with People, Readings, Professional Associations, Resources, and Technology*

What resources exist in your school and community that could assist new teachers in collaborating with others?

Directions:

1. Review the answers you both completed in the "What is needed and wanted?" boxes on page 180. What does the new teacher need? What do you want to share? Keep the answers to these questions in mind when you explore possible resources.
2. Copy this Connect page so you both can investigate resources separately. Bring your completed March Plan "What is needed and wanted?" and Connect pages to the next meeting and compare what you both discovered. If you are working with a group of new teachers, make copies of all of their completed Connect pages and distribute the resource ideas to everyone in the group.

CONNECT *with People . . .*

Who in the school building (experienced teachers, other beginning teachers, custodians, secretaries, etc.) may be able to help with March needs?

What agencies in the community should be used as collaborating partners?

How can parents be helpful this month?

CONNECT *with Readings, Professional Associations, and Resources . . .*

What have you read or used that would assist in networking with other adults? New teachers may refer to student teaching courses and readings. Mentors may have books that relate to this topic.

CONNECT *with Technology . . .*

Find websites and links that will provide information about:

- Teacher collaboration
- Teacher leadership
- Collaborating with parents and other community agencies
- The role of business partners in schools
- Teachers teaching teachers
- New teacher support networks

● ACTIVITIES: *Select Topics for Quality Discussions*

What Will We Discuss at Our March Meetings?

Each month begins with a formal first week planning meeting where dates and times for discussions are scheduled. Use the agenda in this chapter to guide your meeting. Select Activity pages listed on this page as possible talking points at this meeting or for any other meetings you schedule during the month. Record your meeting dates and time on your Planning calendar. You may decide to assign some Activity pages to the new teacher for completion alone. Use the Appendix for five-, ten-, fifteen-, twenty-, thirty-, and sixty-minute meeting formats you may want to use during the month.

Schedule this meeting during the first week of the month	**PLAN the Monthly Discussions (see sample agenda)**
✓ The Activities you will discuss	**ACT by Selecting Appropriate Topics for Discussions during the Month**
	Activities for March discussions related to *Collaboration* include . . .
	ACT 1 Ways to Provide Feedback
	ACT 2 Preconference Conversation Is a Must
	ACT 3 Observing a New Teacher
	ACT 4 Preparing a New Teacher for a Principal Observation
	ACT 5 Connecting New Teachers to Professional Organizations
	ACT 6 Connecting New Teachers to Community Resources
	* ACT 7 Classroom and Behavior Management Issues
	* ACT 8 Looking at Student Work
	* ACT 9 Communicating with Parents
	* ACT 10 Observing New Teachers
	* ACT 11 Preparing a Professional Portfolio
The last day of the month the new teachers and you complete these pages on your own.	**REFLECT and SET GOALS for Next Month** **Give new teachers copies of REFLECT and SET GOALS pages to bring to the April first week meeting.**

*These five Activities will be offered each month from January through June

First Week Agenda: Making a Plan for the Month

TOPIC: Collaborating with New Teachers: Observing and Building a Trusting Relationship

Have snacks and water or soft drinks available. Hold the meeting in your classroom or another comfortable space where you will be sure you will not be interrupted. Put a colorful sign on your door that says "Mentoring Meeting—Please do not disturb."

First: Welcome and introductions: Invite new teachers to share something that is going well.

Then: Review the February new teacher Reflections.

- How did the new teachers respond? How will this impact what you do next?
- Share any of your Mentor Reflections that are appropriate.

Next: Review the Set Goals page that you both completed the last day of February.

- How will these goals carry over into this month?
- What do we want to talk about when we meet this month?
- Share the possible key questions listed at the beginning of this chapter.
- What most interests the new teachers right now?

Begin: Plan what you will discuss this month use the Planning calendar to set your meeting times. Think about how you should share information with the new teachers. Will you give handouts, a tour of your room, or hold discussions? Review the Activities pages for handouts and discussion ideas. Use the Appendix for five-, ten-, fifteen-, twenty-, thirty-, and sixty-minute meeting templates. Modify Activities and templates as needed.

Network: Complete the Connections page together.

Acknowledge: Recognize what you and the new teachers have done so far instead of focusing on what they don't know. Remind the new teachers that they will complete Reflections and Set Goals pages on their own the last day of the month to bring to the first week meeting the next month.

Share: End the session with compliments for each new teacher and at least one practical idea related to collaboration with colleagues and other adults. Let new teachers share ideas about what is working for them.

Ways to Provide Feedback

New teachers want to know how they are doing. They like praise, but need specifics to continue practices that actually have an impact on student learning. Sometimes they don't know what they are doing right, because they spend so much time seeing what is wrong. Giving feedback to new teachers is a delicate area. It has to be respectful, of course, and allow the new teacher to grow from the information you are giving. Sometimes mentors offer suggestions that work in their classrooms, but new teachers are uncomfortable with those suggestions. When they don't implement them, some mentors feel that their feedback is not being used and thus stop giving it.

Before giving any feedback to a new teacher, you need to think about the ways you have received feedback in the past. How did it make you feel? What types of feedback are useful to you? Do you like written feedback so you can think about it later? Do you prefer to have an informal conversation or a formal sit down meeting? Your reflections will provide a lens through which to understand how a new teacher is feeling. The key is to *ask* the new teachers how they would like their feedback and then do it their way. A good mentor understands what is needed and wanted.

	Verbal	Written	Other
Informal Unplanned	✓ Talking after a lesson ✓ Seeing each other in the hallway ✓ A five-minute compliment meeting (see Appendix)	A written note put into the new teacher's mailbox	Putting the names of the new teachers in the school newspaper
Informal Planned	✓ Any meetings from Appendix for ten, fifteen, twenty, thirty minutes	A dialogue journal that you and the new teacher keep	Audiotaping for the new teacher and listening together
Formal Planned	✓ The first meeting of the month	Data collected at formal observations	Videotaping a lesson and discussing it

Preconference Conversation Is a Must

An observation cycle usually consists of (1) a preconference, at which the process is discussed; (2) the observation, when the data are collected; and (3) a postconference for discussion and feedback about the lesson. At the first preconference you should be prepared to do the following:

1. Share the observation techniques* and mutually agree on one you will use to observe the lesson. It's acceptable to be a novice at supervision and to share with the new teacher that you are a novice.
2. Discuss the specific purpose of the observation (e.g., to listen for questions, to look at movement, to videotape and look for facial expression). The more specific you are, the better. The two of you can decide which technique may be suited to the lesson and what particular aspect the new teacher might be interested in learning more about.
3. Have the new teacher share the lesson plan and any aspects of the lesson procedure with you at this time. This may include fears or anxieties about presenting the lesson.
4. Set up a time to have the postconference to review the data collected. List the date here and on your Planning calendar.
5. Decide what you will do with the data after they have been collected and reviewed.

*The observation techniques on the next page will guide you if you are new at this.

Observing a New Teacher

Use any of the techniques on this page to collect data about what the new teacher is doing and how the students are responding. After the data is collected, sit together and discuss one specific thing that would improve the new teacher's practice and his or her students' learning. Acknowledge what is going well and set a date to check in on the goal's progress.

- *Scripting.* Writing everything you say or do during the lesson. This is a profile of the lesson in narrative form.
- *Verbal Feedback.* Listening to your speaking as it relates to asking questions, giving praise, talk time, reprimanding, or gender.
- *Movement.* Recording how you move around the room or how students interact with you, or both.
- *Timing.* Recording the time it takes for introduction, giving directions, answering questions, doing assignments, and cleaning up.
- *Audiotaping.* Providing equipment and taping you for voice, articulation, directions, or any specific aspect of speech.
- *Videotaping.* Recording a lesson and observing the lesson together with nonjudgmental questions prepared.

Preparing a New Teacher for a Principal Observation

New teachers most likely will have had the principal in their room before March, but usually March is when decisions have to be made about rehiring. This evaluation may have more weight on the decision, because principals want to see how the teacher has grown up to this point. As a mentor you will not be involved in the evaluation process; however, you can be a coach for the new teacher and provide him or her with some tips for success.

Here are some you may want to share and add your own ideas.

Before the Observation . . .

- Remind the new teachers that the purpose of the principal's observation is to assess, not to criticize. The principal can learn a lot about the teacher and his or her students in that one visit.
- Write the objective of the lesson on the board and how it relates to the school standards. What will the students be learning in this lesson and why are they learning this?
- Talk to other new teachers who have been observed to find out what the format of the observation will be.
- Meet with the administrator in advance to share the lesson plan and find out what will be expected during the observation.
- Plan the lesson completely and be sure that all materials and supplies are in place.
- Organize and clean the classroom so the principal can walk around student desks.
- Make a list of possible things that could go wrong and discuss them with other new teachers or mentors.

During the Observation . . .

- Be yourself and forget that the principal is in the room (if you can!).
- Remember you are not perfect and you are willing to learn from feedback during the postconference.

After the Observation . . .

- Write down your thoughts about how the lesson went and what you think could be better (you may want to use the self-evaluation form from a previous chapter).
- Set up a postconference meeting with the principal.
- Listen to the feedback and share your perspective.
- Don't defend your actions; rather, be open to suggestions and new learning.
- After the meeting write, in your journal what you learned about yourself in this process.

Connecting New Teachers to Professional Organizations

There are many organizations for teachers today, with focuses ranging from early childhood to secondary subjects. These organizations have local, state, and national conferences and workshops. Most have a professional journal that keeps you updated on current research and practice. Check with your school librarian to find out which organizations the school may already be a member of and which journals are in the library for your use. Share this information at one of your meetings.

Some Professional Organizations

- Association of Supervision and Curriculum Development
- Association for Early Childhood Education
- International Reading Association
- National Council for Social Studies
- National Council of Teachers of English
- National Council of Teachers of Mathematics
- National Science Teachers Association

In addition, a weekly education newspaper called *Education Week* highlights national and state news related to education issues.

A variety of teacher magazines also provide practical tips, teacher talk columns, units, lesson plans, and hands-on ideas. Check with your local school library for details.

Which journals, organizations, or magazines appeal to you? ____________________

Professional Teachers Unions

The two large general professional organizations are the National Education Association (NEA) and the American Federation of Teachers (AFT). The NEA was formed to promote professional development and improve teaching practices through collective bargaining. The AFT functions primarily as a labor union to raise salaries and improve working conditions. Your school district may be associated with either the NEA or the AFT through its state affiliate. Talk with the union members in your school to find out more about the professional opportunities available through the teachers associations.

What are the benefits for teacher members? ______________________________

Connecting New Teachers to Community Resources

Experienced teachers have found the places in the community that give free paper to teachers or that come in to classrooms to be guest speakers. Share these connections with the new teachers. They shouldn't have to wait for years to find these valuable connections.

- *Who are the people in the community new teachers should know?*

  Newspaper editor?

  Reporter?

  Fire chief?

  Chamber of Commerce president?

- *What public agencies could provide support?*

  Public library?

  YMCA or YWCA? Boys and Girls Clubs?

  Police programs for public safety talks?

  Elderly agencies for reading tutors?

- *What businesses have supported public education?*

  Food donations for snacks for students?

  Supplies for classrooms?

- *What other resources do you have that would assist these new teachers?*

Classroom and Behavior Management Issues

Individual Conference Reports

If new teachers are having difficulty with one student, encourage them to meet with the student privately to discuss the issue. Use a conference report like the one on this page to document the conversation and to let the student know that this is a formal meeting. Speaking to misbehaving students in front of their peers and continually reprimanding them probably is not working if the new teachers are still doing it in March. The conference report system provides documentation if further action is required by the teacher.

Conference Report

Student's Name: ______________________________ Date: ______________

Reason for Conference: ______________________________

Summary of Conference: ______________________________

____

____

____

____

____

Signature of Teacher ______________________________

Signature of Student ______________________________

Looking at Student Work

What Should the Teacher Do Next?

Use the same work samples from February and review the completed table. Add the column entitled, "What does the new teacher need to do to move this student to the next level of performance?"

Student	List several skills student is not meeting.	What is ONE skill the student could focus on next to improve learning?	What does the new teacher need to do to move the student to the next level of learning?
#1	See February	See February	
#2	See February	See February	
#3	See February	See February	
#4	See February	See February	

Discuss any patterns or trends that emerge in the new teachers' discussion about what one thing they need to do next with each of these students.

Communicating with Parents

There are a variety of ways in which new teachers can collaborate with parents and other adults in the community to assist them in helping their students make progress. If the school or district has a formal program for this type of collaboration, share this information with your new teachers now. Here are some ideas the new teachers could do on their own in addition to or instead of district programs.

Parent Workshop and Lecture Nights

If you have every done this, share how it works. Usually several teachers at a school organize a workshop around a topic such as math or reading. Secondary teachers may ask a guest speaker to talk about a specific topic. The purpose of the event is for the parents to learn the content so they can either help their children at home or just have a better understanding of what their children are learning in school. Students come to the event with their parents and do the workshop together. So an elementary math night would allow the students and their parents to learn about fractions together. The students get to show off a bit, too! A secondary history lecture about World War II would be a professional activity the parents and students could hear together.

Business Partnerships

In some school districts formal business partners come into the school and tutor students or read to them every Friday. New teachers could find a business sponsor and use the adults in the community as resources to help students in their classrooms. It is a win–win for the community and the students. The partnerships could also provide guest speakers and resources. Many businesses update equipment and paper supplies and would love to donate to a school. New teachers need these connections because they are just building up their classroom resources.

Alumni Mentoring Program

Graduates of local high schools often like to come back to mentor students at risk. If they successfully completed a college program and have made a successful life, these students want to share it. Create a way for these new teachers to tap into the graduates of the district and assist in matching them with at-risk students in elementary and secondary classrooms. Graduating from high school is important today, and the dropout rate is growing because of failure on high-stakes tests. Mentoring may help, and it can begin early.

Observing New Teachers

If you are fortunate enough to have release time to observe any new teachers, you may find this feedback form useful. A preconference and a postconference will also provide structure to your comments. Remember your feedback is just that . . . it does not mean the new teachers have to accept it or use it. Don't take it personally if they don't.

Feedback Form

Date: ______________________________

Subject/Grade: ______________________________

Title of Lesson: ______________________________

1. How well was the lesson plan written? Was it clear and easy to follow? Did it have a purpose that related to student learning?

2. How well did the new teacher carry out the lesson plan's objectives?

3. Describe one positive aspect of the lesson that demonstrates the new teacher's skills as a beginning teacher.

4. How were the students engaged during the lesson to encourage learning?

Commendations (positive aspects of teaching demonstrated):

Recommendations (suggestions for future lessons):

Other comments:

Preparing a Professional Portfolio

In January (ACT 3) new teachers were invited to describe their qualities. Have the new teachers do the process again and compare their answers to that process. They can use their current answers as the basis for a one-page philosophy statement for their portfolios. The examples of the teaching experiences will become important pages that will demonstrate what they are teaching. Encourage the new teachers to take photographs.

1. How have your descriptive words of yourself changed?

   New words you would use to describe yourself:

   ____________________, ____________________, ____________________

2. How have your beliefs changed?

   New beliefs you now hold about teaching and learning:

____

____

____

3. List as many concrete examples as you can that relate to the description and beliefs you have written:

____

____

____

After you have compared your philosophy statements and added any new words use these ideas to write the one-page philosophy statement for the front page of your portfolio. This statement will be the foundation of your portfolio. All artifacts and examples will stem from this platform statement. Remember that your statement will be unique and will represent who you are as a teacher and how you see yourself.

● REFLECT *on This Month's Discussions*

Mentor's Reflections

Directions: Complete as many of the bubble prompts as you would like after you have finished the Activites in the chapter and before you Set Goals. Add your own prompts to blank bubbles if these prompts do not meet your needs. Ask your new teachers to complete their own reflection bubbles on the next page. Compare and share your reflections at one of your meetings. You may consider using one or two reflection bubbles as topics for future mentoring discussions.

I would like to have the new teachers observe me teach . . .
A professional conference or meeting I would like to share with my new teachers . . .
I would like to connect my new teachers with the following adults . . .
I am surprised by . . .

New Teachers' Reflections

Directions: Complete as many of the bubble prompts as you would like after you have finished the Activities in the chapter and before you Set Goals. Add your own prompts to blank bubbles if the prompts listed do not meet your needs. Compare and share your reflections with your mentor and other new teachers at a scheduled meeting.

The best thing that happened this month is . . .

The thing that has helped me the most this year is . . .

Something I would like to see my mentor teach is . . .

I would like to________________ with my mentor . . .

● SET GOALS *for Next Month*

Directions:

- Complete this Set Goals page the last day of the month after your Reflection and use it to guide the First Week meeting for next month.
- Review the PLAN–CONNECT–ACT pages you completed in this chapter to see what you need to revisit next month based on the new teachers' needs. List two needs that stand out for you right now.
- Ask yourself how you would like to share what the new teachers need with them.

  Will you give a tour of your classroom?

  Will you share materials you have made?

  Will you take them to the library and show them how to use existing resources?

  Will you connect them with people who can assist them regularly?

  What will you do to be an effective mentor?
- List two goals for yourself as a mentor for next month. How do your goals relate to what observe the new teachers' top two needs to be?

New Teacher Needs **(from reflections, conversations, and your observations)**	**Your Mentor Goals**
1.	1.
2.	2.

A good teacher goes to teacher school. —First-Grade Student

Standards

Creating Meaningful Standards-Based Learning Experiences for Students

New Teacher Phase: Confusion

"How can I teach what is important and also meet the district standards for high-stakes tests?"

INTASC Principles

Revisit INTASC Principles 1 through 7.

- **PRINCIPLE 1 Making Content Meaningful** (see October chapter)
- **PRINCIPLE 2 Child Development and Learning Theory** (see September chapter)
- **PRINCIPLE 3 Learning Styles/Diversity** (see November chapter)
- **PRINCIPLE 4 Instructional Strategies/Problem Solving** (see December chapter)
- **PRINCIPLE 5 Motivation and Behavior** (see September chapter)
- **PRINCIPLE 6 Communication/Knowledge** (see February chapter)
- **PRINCIPLE 7 Planning for Instruction** (see October chapter)

Standards

Creating Meaningful Standards-Based Learning Experiences for Students

The first-grade student who said "A good teacher goes to teacher school" really knew something. The new teachers with whom you are working, who were prepared in schools of education where they took courses in content and pedagogy, should have some understanding of standards. Some of your new teachers may have entered the profession by alternate routes and thus have not had prior experiences through teacher education programs. As a mentor, you probably have noticed the difference in the needs of these two groups of teachers. Differentiated mentoring is needed to be able to accommodate the needs of both groups.

This chapter focuses on standards because they relate to the high-stakes standardized tests that are currently being used to measure student progress. At this point in time many new teachers get confused. They were prepared to teach one way in schools of education that focused on student learning, and now they are told the students must pass these tests. How can the new teachers do both? Do they have to teach to the test to meet the passing rates? What should they do? Every district and school is wrestling with this dilemma. Of course, proponents of the tests say just teach the way you teach and the students will pass. Teachers are finding there is a disconnect between the models of learning they were taught and the test-taking skills required to do well. Discuss this dilemma with the new teachers.

Use the pages this month to . . . Plan your monthly meetings by deciding what you would like to talk about as well as to set meeting dates for the month, think about how you will Connect your new teachers to available resources, select Activities that make sense for you to discuss, Reflect at the end of the month, and Set Goals for next month. Use all of these process pages as a guide to enrich the quality of your monthly mentoring conversations.

What Do We Want to Talk about When We Meet This Month?

Invite your new teachers to write down a short list of questions and bring them to your first April meeting. Use the questions below as a guide for your discussions throughout the month.

New Teachers' Possible Questions:

1. Can you review with me how to make content meaningful?
2. My students seem to be changing at this time of year. I need help remembering my adolescent and child psychology. Is this supposed to be happening, or are my students different?
3. The diversity in my room is overwhelming. I have so many learning styles. What can I do?
4. Instructional strategies for diverse learners are important, but I find myself teaching the whole class the same way. Do you have any suggestions?
5. The behavior in my room is really challenging. I need a refresher. Are there any support systems for me right now?
6. I am trying to communicate in different ways with my students. Can you review them with me to be sure I am on track?
7. I don't have time to plan the way I did in the fall. I know that when I do, the day goes much better, but I just can't fit everything in. Can you help me get organized?

List the other questions your new teachers brought to the meeting so you will have them for your next mentoring cycle.

As a Mentor, You Can Ask Questions, Too!

Try to ask more questions to learn about your new teachers, rather than telling them how things should be done.

Mentor's Possible Question:

What can I do to assist you right now that would reduce your anxiety?

● PLAN *Agendas and Schedule Meetings*

Plan your monthly meetings, decide when and how you want to Connect with each other as well as others in the school and community, select the Activities from this chapter that make sense for you to discuss, Reflect separately at the end of the end of the month and share your reflection, and Set Goals for next month.

PLAN *Agendas for Monthly Meetings Based on New Teacher Needs*

Planning quality conversations means that the needs of the new teacher must be met. Take time to complete the chart before making decisions about what you will discuss at your monthly mentoring sessions. What makes most sense for you as a mentor to share in April?

Complete this together and save for future discussion. Make a copy for the new teacher if needed.

What is needed and wanted in April?

New Teacher *I need . . .*	Mentor *I want to share . . .*

When Will We Meet?

Plan to meet at times that allow you to have quality time together without interruptions. Knowing when you will meet reduces anxiety for both of you all month. New teachers look forward to planned meetings.

When will you meet?

How many times during the month?

How long will you meet for quality conversations? Ten, twenty, or thirty minutes? Indicate that on this calendar.

Will your new teacher observe you teach and demonstrate a skill this month?

Will you observe the new teacher(s) this month? Purpose of the observation is . . .

Are there other teachers or community members your new teacher(s) need to connect with this month? Indicate on this schedule.

Make a copy of this calendar for each new teacher. Also put these times into your teaching plan book.

April Calendar

MONDAY	TUESDAY	WEDNESDAY	THURSDAY	FRIDAY

Key: B = before school D = during the day (preparation time or lunch time) A = After school

CONNECT *with People, Readings, Professional Associations, Resources, and Technology*

What resources exist in your school and community that could assist new teachers in creating meaningful standards-based learning experiences?

Directions:

1. Review the answers you both completed in the "What is needed and wanted?" boxes on page 202. What does the new teacher need? What do you want to share? Keep the answers to these questions in mind when you explore possible resources.
2. Copy this Connect page so you both can investigate resources separately. Bring your completed April Plan "What is needed and wanted?" and Connect pages to the next meeting and compare what you both discovered. If you are working with a group of new teachers, make copies of all of their completed Connect pages and distribute the resource ideas to everyone in the group.

CONNECT *with People . . .*

Who in the school building (experienced teachers, other beginning teachers, custodians, secretaries, etc.) may be able to help with April needs?

What district departments relate to testing and curriculum?

How can parents be helpful in assisting around curriculum and testing issues?

CONNECT *with Readings, Professional Associations, and Resources . . .*

What have you read or used that would assist learning more about curriculum, testing, and standards. New teachers may refer to student teaching courses and readings. Mentors may have books or district documents that relate to this topic.

CONNECT *with Technology . . .*

Find websites and links that will provide information about:

- All INTASC principles
- State and local standards
- District curriculum frameworks
- Testing policies and mandates
- No Child Left Behind Act

● ACTIVITIES: *Select Topics for Quality Discussions*

What Will We Discuss at Our April Meetings?

Each month begins with a formal first week planning meeting where dates and times for discussions are scheduled. Use the agenda in this chapter to guide your meeting. Select Activity pages listed on this page as possible talking points at this meeting or for any other meetings you schedule during the month. Record your meeting dates and time on your Planning calendar. You may decide to assign some Activity pages to the new teacher for completion alone. Use the Appendix for five-, ten-, fifteen-, twenty-, thirty-, and sixty-minute meeting formats you may want to use during the month.

Schedule this meeting during the first week of the month	**PLAN the Monthly Discussions (see sample agenda)**
✓ The Activities you will discuss	**ACT by Selecting Appropriate Topics for Discussions during the Month**
	Activities for April discussions related to *Standards* include . . .
	ACT 1 Relating Classroom Curriculum to District Standards
	ACT 2 TTT versus STT
	ACT 3 Relating Standards to Real Life
	ACT 4 Observing an Individual Student
	ACT 5 Observing a Small Group
	* ACT 6 Classroom and Behavior Management Issues
	* ACT 7 Looking at Student Work
	* ACT 8 Communicating with Parents
	* ACT 9 Observing New Teachers
	* ACT 10 Preparing a Professional Portfolio
	ACT 11 New Teacher Needs
The last day of the month the new teachers and you complete these pages on your own.	**REFLECT and SET GOALS for Next Month** **Give new teachers copies of REFLECT and SET GOALS pages to bring to the May first week meeting.**

*These five Activities will be offered each month from January through June.

● *First Week Agenda: Making a Plan for the Month*

TOPIC: Standards: Creating Meaningful Standards-Based Learning Experiences

Have snacks and water or soft drinks available. Hold the meeting in your classroom or another comfortable space where you will be sure you will not be interrupted. Put a colorful sign on your door that says "Mentoring Meeting—Please do not disturb."

First: Welcome and introductions: Invite new teachers to share something that is going well.

Then: Review the March new teacher Reflections.

- How did the new teachers respond? How will this impact what you do next?
- Share any of your mentor Reflections that are appropriate.

Next: Review the Set Goals page that you both completed the last day of March.

- How will these goals carry over into this month?
- What do we want to talk about when we meet this month?
- Share the possible key questions listed at the beginning of this chapter.
- What most interests the new teachers right now?

Begin: Plan what you will discuss this month use the Planning calendar to set your meeting times. Think about how you should share information with the new teachers. Will you give handouts, a tour of your room, or hold discussions? Review the Activities pages for handouts and discussion ideas. Use the Appendix for five-, ten-, fifteen-, twenty-, thirty-, and sixty-minute meeting templates. Modify Activities and templates as needed.

Network: Complete the Connections page together.

Acknowledge: Recognize what you and the new teachers have done so far instead of focusing on what they don't know. Remind the new teachers that they will complete Reflections and Set Goals pages on their own the last day of the month to bring to the first week meeting the next month.

Share: End the session with compliments for each new teacher and at least one practical idea related to preparing students for standardized tests. Let new teachers share ideas about what is working for them.

Relating Classroom Curriculum to District Standards

Discuss the ways standards are made explicit in the new teacher's classroom. If you are working with a small group of new teachers, invite them to bring examples of standards-based lessons. Use the following questions as a guide for your discussions. Remind the new teachers that standards are not activities. Many new teachers get excited about "doing activities" with their students but then have difficulty relating what they are doing to a standard.

Lesson Plan Discussion

This process can be done prior to teaching a lesson so the new teacher can modify or after a lesson has been taught so the new teacher can reflect and make changes for future lesson plans.

1. What is the purpose of this lesson?

2. Why are you teaching this?

3. Why now?

4. Is it part of a larger unit of study?

5. Which standards relate to this lesson?

6. Why did you select them?

7. How do you think students will respond to this lesson?

8. Will all learners be engaged? How will you know?

9. Is there any aspect of your lesson you anticipate may be challenging? Why?

10. What is the most valuable part of this lesson that relates to learning?

TTT versus STT (Teacher Talking Time versus Student Talking Time)

An excellent soccer coach once said that you make a good player by giving him or her as many "touches on the ball" as possible during every practice session. Teachers who talk the whole lesson and never let the students talk or engage in the curriculum are like coaches who tell the players how to do it, but never let them practice. Encourage the new teachers with whom you are working to notice how much time they are talking during any lesson and how much time they allow the students to talk to each other as they engage in meaningful learning activities. Encourage your new teachers to give their students "many touches on the ball"!

Review the responses to February ACT 4 to begin this discussion. New teachers use their voices all day long in many different ways. Some relate to learning and others do not. When do student voices get heard?

How can new teachers increase appropriate Student Talking Time?

- Integrate paired sharing into lessons
- Allow time for discussion in lessons
- Begin each class with time for students to share what they already know about a topic
- End a class with time to share what they learned today
- Partner English language learners with native speakers
- Include read-aloud activities in lessons
- Your ideas!

Emphasize that the talking needs to relate to learning objectives that relate to the standards. New teachers need to be mindful at all times of what they are teaching and why. Allowing student learners to talk in class is one way to keep them alert and engaged. Just like in soccer, players who are on the field have to be engaged. The students won't be bored and are less likely to misbehave if they are "playing" in the game.

Relating Standards to Real Life

Connecting your students through the existing curriculum is a better way to include service than adding on another activity for already busy students. Service learning engages students and makes the curriculum come alive for all learners. Service projects can also be offered as enrichment, extra credit, and homework for those students who are committed to make a difference.

New teachers can use the community to make the standards come alive for their students. Assist them in finding ways their students can participate in "service learning" in the community. What can you add to the list below? Take time to have new teachers make the standard explicit to the new teachers and their students. What are they supposed to know and be able to do as a result of this service?

Examples of service learning activities:

History, middle/high	Interview and audiotape World War II veterans and then have them come to the classroom as guest speakers. Provide a service to the local veteran's association as part of this activity.
Science, middle/high	Connect with a recycling center on a project that relates to the science chapter on recycling.
Elementary	Write to elderly and visit them on holidays; use as language arts.
Elementary, middle, high	Volunteer at a shelter or soup kitchen and write about the experience.
Elementary	Invite local businesses into the classroom while learning about professions and select one that needs a special project completed.

Other ideas?

____

____

____

Why is it important to have students make the connection between learning information and service learning?

Observing an Individual Student

At this time of year each new teacher will have at least one student who is a challenge. It is easy to blame the student—after all, the student is the one acting out. Encourage your new teachers to be more clinical and less personal in their approach to observing the students who are challenging. Using the format below, encourage each new teacher to use his or her observation skills, without judgment, to delve deeper into this student's world. Thinking like an ethnographer, instead of a teacher, the exercise may bring new evidence to the surface that may assist the new teacher in working with this student for the rest of the year. The new teacher may need to do this process more than once.

First Name of Student: ______________________ Date of Observation: ____________

Challenge This Student Presents:

1. What do you notice about this student (physical appearance, cultural background, language, social interaction, skills and abilities, motivation, attitude, self-concept, etc.)

2. How is the student responding to the teacher's lesson?

3. Is the student interacting with any other students? Describe.

4. What is the quality of the student's work?

5. Name something positive the student did during the lesson.

6. What other things did you observe that you didn't know about the student?

Observing a Small Group

New teachers are encouraged to group their students to enhance learning, but often grouping students creates behavior problems. So what is a new teacher to do? Not grouping leaves students bored and teachers doing all the talking, yet grouping may be too challenging. Encourage new teachers to observe a small group in action and see what works and what doesn't.

After your new teachers have stepped back and observed a group using the following questions as a guide, assist them in creating student ground rules for working in groups. All group work should relate to a curriculum standard and not just be busy work.

1. Why is this small group working together?

2. Who is the leader of the group? Self-appointed or teacher-appointed?

3. How effective is the leader?

4. Is the group completing the assigned task? How do you know?

5. Are all members of the group participating? What are the differences in the individual members' contributions to the group? Give an example.

6. What is your overall impression of this group activity?

Classroom and Behavior Management Issues

Student Contract

At this time of the year, students will be testing the patience and skills of new teachers. Sometimes it helps to have the student state in writing how he or she will change the behavior that has been so disruptive. Here is a model. Invite the new teachers to invent their own. The key here is having the students write how their success will be measured. How will the new teacher know the student has changed? Also the reward is important and the new teacher should add by when __________ (date) or else the reward expires!

Student Contract

I state that I will *(change a certain behavior)* ______________________________

______________________________.

I will measure my success by *(how the behavior will be noted as being done)* ______________________________

______________________________.

For successful demonstration *(I will receive a reward)* ______________________________

______________________________.

Signed (teacher) ______________________________ Date ______________

Signed (student) ______________________________ Date ______________

The contract can also be designed for groups by changing *I* to *we*.

Looking at Student Work

What are the students doing right? Ask the new teachers to bring samples of student work to a meeting. After the samples have been sorted into one of the three standards categories (or your own categories), select one sample from each pile.

Below Standard	**Meets the Standard**	**Above Standard**
How many papers here? % of class _____ Select ONE paper: What can this student be complimented for?	How many papers here? % of class _____ Select ONE paper: What can this student be complimented for?	How many papers here? % of class _____ Select ONE paper: What can this student be complimented for?

Discuss why complimenting students is important to improving progress.

Communicating with Parents

Teaching Effective Study Skills

Parents know schoolwork, homework, and tests are important, but they often don't know how to help their children learn. These parents come to meetings with teachers and want to help, they just don't know what to tell their children to do.

Brainstorm ways new teachers can educate parents about effective study habits.

Offer a parent information session in the evening that highlights effective study skills. Actually teach the parents what the new teachers are teaching the students.

Effective Study Skill What is it? Describe the skill.	**Elementary Students** What behavior would parent see?	**Secondary Students** What behavior would parent see?
Homework paper		
Studying for a test		
Reading a chapter and taking notes		

What should parents know and be able to do to help their children learn? Discuss this with the new teachers.

Observing New Teachers

Goal setting is critical to observation. After any observation you have completed with a new teacher, take time to set *one* goal together. Try to figure out an action that, if made by the new teacher, would advance his or her practice. What would that goal be?

GOAL	
ACTIONS What will you do to achieve your goal?	
EVALUATION Date for Goal Review. How will you know if you reach your goal?	

Sample Goals

Having interesting introductions to lessons

Culminating a lesson in an orderly way

Moving around the classroom

Pronouncing all the words in a lesson correctly

Managing an effective classroom routine during a lesson

Make the goal achievable, observable, and measurable!

Preparing a Professional Portfolio

Encourage the new teachers to review the artifacts they have been collecting in their binder or box sometime this month. If they are completing a portfolio for the district review district guidelines, you may review district guidelines now. If they are creating a portfolio for professional display, this is a good time to assist them in organizing their work.

New teachers should select artifacts from their binders and boxes that relate to what they believe about teaching and learning as well as the district standards.

Ask new teachers to . . .

1. Review their philosophy of education and rewrite if needed.
   What do I have that matches what I believe?
   What do I want to make sure is absolutely in my portfolio?
   What is missing that I need to include?
2. Review district or state standards for portfolio submission.
3. Decide on a format (binder, artist portfolio, web etc.).
4. Write the table of contents (based on standards).
5. Continue to collect artifacts (audio and video).
6. Set a deadline for completion.

New Teacher Needs

Review the Plan page in the beginning of this chapter, "What is needed and wanted?" by your new teachers. Create your own Activity for a discussion topic and set aside time to address this issue with your new teacher(s).

What is needed by your new teachers that was not included in the Activities list for this month?

How can you help the new teacher in this area?

Who can you refer the new teacher to for additional support?

As you begin to think about closing the school year with your new teachers, think about what you know that they may not know yet. How can you help?

● REFLECT *on This Month's Discussions*

Mentor's Reflections

Directions: Complete as many of the bubble prompts as you would like after you have finished the Activities in the chapter and before you Set Goals. Add your own prompts to blank bubbles if these prompts do not meet your needs. Ask your new teachers to complete their own reflection bubbles on the next page. Compare and share your reflections at one of your meetings. You may consider using one or two reflection bubbles as topics for future mentoring discussions.

A goal I need to work on with the new teachers is . . .
The new teachers are learning . . .
An area of growth I have observed is . . .
What I am learning about mentoring is . . .

New Teachers' Reflections

Directions: Complete as many of the bubble prompts as you would like after you have finished the Activities in the chapter and before you Set Goals. Add your own prompts to blank bubbles if the prompts listed do not meet your needs. Compare and share your reflections with your mentor and other new teachers at a scheduled meeting.

I am frustrated by . . .

One thing that would make a difference is . . .

Teaching is . . .

I see myself teaching . . .

● SET GOALS *for Next Month*

Directions:

- Complete this Set Goals page the last day of the month after your Reflection and use it to guide the first week meeting for next month.
- Review the PLAN–CONNECT–ACT pages you completed in this chapter to see what you need to revisit next month based on the new teachers' needs. List two needs that stand out for you right now.
- Ask yourself how you would like to share what the new teachers need with them.

  Will you give a tour of your classroom?

  Will you share materials you have made?

  Will you take them to the library and show them how to use existing resources?

  Will you connect them with people who can assist them regularly?

  What will you do to be an effective mentor?
- List two goals for yourself as a mentor for next month. How do your goals relate to what observe the new teachers' top two needs to be?

New Teacher Needs (from reflections, conversations, and your observations)	Your Mentor Goals
1.	1.
2.	2.

Good teachers listen to their students and care how their students are doing academically. —High School Student

Assessing Students' Progress

High-Stakes Tests and Teacher Assessment

New Teacher Phase: Hope

"It looks like my students are passing tests and learning. Maybe I can do this."

INTASC Principles

Revisit INTASC Principle 8.

- **PRINCIPLE 8 Assessment**
  The teacher understands and uses formal and informal assessment strategies to evaluate and ensure the continuous intellectual, social, and physical development of the learner.

Assessing Students' Progress

High Stakes Tests and Teacher Assessment

Good teachers care about how their students are doing academically, said one high school student. Teachers who are trying to help students learn, as opposed to giving tests and recording scores, make more points with students. As a mentor, you can assess the kind of teachers you are working with. Do they care about how the students are doing because it is a reflection on them, or do they care because they want the students to succeed in school and life?

At this time of the year new teachers need be hopeful. Some of their students are passing the tests, and it actually looks like students did learn something this year. The new teachers may be thinking, perhaps I *can* do this after all. The phases of the year do bring them up and down. The INTASC Principle 8 (Assessment) focuses on both formal and informal assessments. High-stakes tests are not the only measure of success. ACT 1 encourages you to discuss the multiple measures of assessment a teacher needs to use to document progress. Learning is developmental, and all students do not learn the identified curriculum the year it is listed in the syllabus. Some learn it later.

Hope is the quality that highlights the service aspect of teaching. Teachers, both new and experienced, hope for the best for their students. They hope what they are doing makes a difference. You hope you are mentoring them effectively. Hope is positive and allows new teaches to sustain their energy to create new goals for their students. Keep that hope alive in the new teachers this month.

Use the pages this month to . . . Plan your monthly meetings by deciding what you would like to talk about as well as to set meeting dates for the month, think about how you will Connect your new teachers to available resources, select Activities that make sense for you to discuss, Reflect at the end of the month, and Set Goals for next month. Use all of these process pages as a guide to enrich the quality of your monthly mentoring conversations.

What Do We Want to Talk about When We Meet This Month?

Invite your new teachers to write down a short list of questions and bring them to your first May meeting. Use the questions below as a guide for your discussions throughout the month.

New Teachers' Possible Questions:

1. How do I grade these students at the end of the year?
2. High-stakes tests are taking so much time. How do I fit in my teaching?
3. What end-of-the year assessments do I need to know?
4. How do you think I am doing?

List the other questions your new teachers brought to the meeting so you will have them for your next mentoring cycle.

As a Mentor, You Can Ask Questions, Too!

Try to ask more questions to learn about your new teachers, rather than telling them how things should be done.

Mentor's Possible Questions:

1. What do you need to do right now?
2. What paperwork do you need to discuss?
3. What can I do to assist you right now that would reduce your anxiety?

● *PLAN Agendas and Schedule Meetings*

Plan your monthly meetings, decide when and how you want to Connect with each other as well as others in the school and community, select the Activities from this chapter that make sense for you to discuss, Reflect separately at the end of the end of the month and share your reflection, and Set Goals for next month.

PLAN *Agendas for Monthly Meetings Based on New Teacher Needs*

Planning quality conversations means that the needs of the new teacher must be met. Take time to complete the chart before making decisions about what you will discuss at your monthly mentoring sessions. What makes most sense for you as a mentor to share in May?

Complete this together and save for future discussion. Make a copy for each new teacher if needed.

What is needed and wanted in May?

New Teacher *I need . . .*	Mentor *I want to share . . .*

When Will We Meet?

Plan to meet at times that allow you to have quality time together without interruptions. Knowing when you will meet reduces anxiety for both of you all month. New teachers look forward to planned meetings.

When will you meet?

How many times during the month?

How long will you meet for quality conversations? Ten, twenty, or thirty minutes? Indicate that on this calendar.

Will your new teacher observe you teach and demonstrate a skill this month?

Will you observe the new teacher(s) this month? Purpose of the observation is . . .

Are there other teachers or community members your new teacher(s) need to connect with this month? Indicate on this schedule.

Make a copy of this calendar for each new teacher. Also put these times into your teaching plan book.

May Calendar

MONDAY	TUESDAY	WEDNESDAY	THURSDAY	FRIDAY

Key: B = before school D = during the day (preparation time or lunch time) A = After school

• CONNECT *with People, Readings, Professional Associations, Resources, and Technology*

What resources exist in your school and community that could assist new teachers in assessing student's progress?

Directions:

1. Review the answers you both completed in the "What is needed and wanted?" boxes on page 224. What does the new teacher need? What do you want to share? Keep the answers to these questions in mind when you explore possible resources.
2. Copy this Connect page so you both can investigate resources separately. Bring your completed May Plan "What is needed and wanted?" and Connect pages to the next meeting and compare what you both discovered. If you are working with a group of new teachers, make copies of all of their completed Connect pages and distribute the resource ideas to everyone in the group.

CONNECT *with People . . .*

Who in the school building (experienced teachers, other beginning teachers, custodians, secretaries, etc.) may be able to help with May needs?

What district departments relate to assessing student progress and referrals for next year?

How are parents included in end of the year student assessments?

CONNECT *with Readings, Professional Associations, and Resources . . .*

What have you read or used that would assist understanding high-stakes tests and district assessment policies? New teachers may refer to student teaching courses and readings. Mentors may district materials that relate to this topic.

CONNECT *with Technology . . .*

Find websites and links that will provide information about:

- High-stakes tests
- Retaining students
- End of the year assessments and evaluation
- District policies
- Formal and informal assessments

● ACTIVITIES: *Select Topics for Quality Discussions*

What Will We Discuss at Our May Meetings?

Each month begins with a formal first week planning meeting where dates and times for discussions are scheduled. Use the agenda in this chapter to guide your meeting. Select Activity pages listed on this page as possible talking points at this meeting or for any other meetings you schedule during the month. Record your meeting dates and time on your Planning calendar. You may decide to assign some Activity pages to the new teacher for completion alone. Use the Appendix for five-, ten-, fifteen-, twenty-, thirty-, and sixty-minute meeting formats you may want to use during the month.

Schedule this meeting during the first week of the month	**PLAN the Monthly Discussions (see sample agenda)**
✓ The Activities you will discuss	**ACT by Selecting Appropriate Topics for Discussions during the Month**
	ACTivities for May discussions related to *Testing and Assessment* include . . .
	ACT 1 Assessing Students' Progress
	* ACT 2 Classroom and Behavior Management Issues
	* ACT 3 Looking at Student Work
	* ACT 4 Communicating with Parents
	* ACT 5 Observing New Teachers
	* ACT 6 Preparing a Professional Portfolio
	ACT 7 New Teacher Needs
The last day of the month the new teachers and you complete these pages on your own.	**REFLECT and SET GOALS for Next Month** **Give new teachers copies of REFLECT and SET GOALS pages to bring to the June first week meeting.**

*These five Activities will be offered each month from January through June.

May

● First Week Agenda: Making a Plan for the Month

TOPIC: Assessing Students' Progress: High-Stakes Tests and Teacher Tests

Have snacks and water or soft drinks available. Hold the meeting in your classroom or another comfortable space where you will be sure you will not be interrupted. Put a colorful sign on your door that says "Mentoring Meeting—Please do not disturb."

First: Welcome and introductions: Invite new teachers to share something that is going well.

Then: Review the April new teacher Reflections.

- How did the new teachers respond? How will this impact what you do next?
- Share any of your mentor Reflections that are appropriate.

Next: Review the Set Goals page that you both completed the last day of April.

- How will these goals carry over into this month?
- What do we want to talk about when we meet this month?
- Share the possible key questions listed at the beginning of this chapter.
- What most interests the new teachers right now?

Begin: Plan what you will discuss this month use the Planning calendar to set your meeting times. Think about how you should share information with the new teachers. Will you give handouts, a tour of your room, or hold discussions? Review the Activities pages for handouts and discussion ideas. Use the Appendix for five-, ten-, fifteen-, twenty-, thirty-, and sixty-minute meeting templates. Modify Activities and templates as needed.

Network: Complete the Connections page together.

Acknowledge: Recognize what you and the new teachers have done so far instead of focusing on what they don't know. Remind the new teachers that they will complete Reflections and Set Goals pages on their own the last day of the month to bring to the first week meeting the next month.

Share: End the session with compliments for each new teacher and at least one practical idea related to testing procedures. Let new teachers share ideas about what is working for them.

Assessing Students' Progress

Discuss all the ways in which a new teacher can assess a student's progress in school. Use the original student profile information collected in September ACT 3 as one way to observe growth and development. Encourage the new teachers to look at multiple measures of growth. How many measures can you think of? View each student as a whole person, not just the result of a test.

- *Student Personal Strengths* (related to the profile in September ACT 3)
  Ability to speak languages
  Musical ability
  Hobbies
  Other
- *Interpersonal and Social Interactions*
  With other students in the classroom
  Leadership qualities
- *Academic Achievement*
  On units of study based on teacher-made tests and quizzes (paper and pencil)
  Project or performance based
- *High-Stakes Testing Results*
  Math
  Literacy
  Other content areas
- *Other valuable information related to this student's progress this year*

Discussion:

How do high-stakes tests relate to overall student learning? or not?

Classroom and Behavior Management Issues

As the year comes to a close, sometimes student misbehavior escalates. Everyone is tired, and the new teachers may have exhausted their ideas. Here are some common sense tips for closing out the year. Add your own and discuss why each one is important to building a community of learners. New teachers may have tried some of these ideas before, but it might be important to have a refresher at this time of the year.

- Focus on positive behavior when it happens.

  Give verbal praise for specific behavior.

  Send notes home with students.

  Make complimentary phone calls to parents about their child.

- Don't threaten or bribe students to behave.

  Students may respond for a short term but will not respect you in the long term, because behavior becomes contingent on continuation of bribe.

- Take charge of the classroom in a firm but pleasant manner.

  Use your sense of humor to keep students in line.

  Communicate your needs honestly to students.

  Listen to your students' requests and complaints.

- Give "I"-messages to students instead of "You"-messages.

  "I am unhappy with the behavior I am seeing," not "You are misbehaving again."

- Use body language and signals to prevent disruptive behavior.

  Make eye contact with the misbehaving student.

  Use frown or facial expression.

  Walk near the student and lightly tap his or her shoulder.

  Use your sense of humor.

  Use a cue to have the students look at you (e.g., lights off, raise hands).

- Don't use sarcasm, cruel remarks, or words to embarrass students.

  No ridicule or intimidation allowed!

  Never touch a student in an abusive way.

  Confrontation in front of a whole class is not recommended.

  If the situation becomes confrontational, remove the student and discuss the problem later.

Looking at Student Work

What Do We Know and Believe about Differentiating Instruction?

Your district probably has workshops on this topic. Some teachers embrace the concept; others are not sure what it means. Others don't believe there should be any differentiation from the standard and that all learners should be treated the same in a same age-level classroom. What you believe as a mentor will impact what the new teachers you are working with believe. Philosophies are personal, but district standards and approaches for student learning are public. How can you discuss the intersection of a teacher's personal belief system and the mandate from the district that all students must learn? We all know that if new teachers don't believe in what "differentiation" stands for, it will be a challenge to have those approaches integrated into their practice. Take the risk, uncover the beliefs.

1. Ask the new teachers what they believe about differentiation and why they believe that.
2. Think about what you will do if a teacher says she does not believe.
3. Share any district materials on this topic. There may have been a workshop for new teachers at some time during their induction year. If so, ask them to bring the materials to your discussion and review them.
4. Discuss specific ways the teachers can differentiate instruction.
5. Look at one sample of student work and differentiate the instruction.

Student	Standard level Below Meets Above	What student needs to learn next	How the teacher could differentiate to assist the student in learning

Communicating with Parents

Student Progress on High-Stakes Tests and Teacher Tests

High-stakes tests are here to stay. In many districts, they mean graduation from high school or not. Teacher-made tests are also part of academic progress, and they serve as the grading system for report cards and moving to the next grade. Both tests are critical to students. So how can parents help? New teachers need to assist parents in understanding the difference between high-stakes and teacher tests and how they both impact their children.

Discuss the ways the district lets parents know about high-stakes tests. Encourage the new teachers with whom you are working to communicate with parents through written material or an information session.

Help the new teachers clarify the differences in the tests and how they are used to measure student progress.

High-Stakes Tests (state or district)	**Teacher-Made Tests (measure of content learned in the classroom)**
(For each type of test) List how it is used and how students benefit from this test.	(For each type of test) List how it is used and how students benefit from this test.

Assist the new teachers in understanding the benefits and limitations of paper-and-pencil testing.

Observing New Teachers

You have been discussing many aspects of new teacher performance this year. Sit with each new teacher and discuss how each would rate him- or herself using this rubric. Define Excellent and Good before you begin the discussion so the new teacher will know how the indicators of progress are defined. What else would you add?

Indicators of excellent progress would be . . .

Indicators of good progress would be . . .

Example of New Teacher Rubric for Instructional Practice

	Excellent Progress	Good Progress	Needs More Development	Needs Assistance	Unsatisfactory
Demonstrates creativity and thought in planning					
Uses a variety of teaching strategies and methods to engage learners					
Develops both long-form and short-form lesson plans					
Demonstrates principles and theories of instruction for students in the classroom					
Demonstrates proper sequencing and pacing of lessons					
Develops and modifies curriculum to meet student needs					
Manages the classroom					
Handles difficult situations through problem-solving approaches					
Maintains an organized classroom for student learning					
Disciplines fairly					

Preparing a Professional Portfolio

A portfolio is not a scrapbook. It is a collection of carefully selected artifacts that tell a story. Assist your new teachers in carefully selecting artifacts that they can use to demonstrate their effectiveness as teachers. Reflecting is a key component to a portfolio. Ask each new teacher to explain why he or she is selecting each artifact.

Step 1: Review all materials collected in the binder or box this year. What stands out as interesting, colorful, and meaningful to share with others?

Step 2: Select key items, photos, samples of student work, notes from parents, for example, that illustrate something the new teacher wants to share. It could be a standard for teaching, a competency, a skill, or an interest. It could also be related to the INTASC standards listed on the cover sheet of each month in this book. Less is more!

Step 3: Write a short description or caption for each item selected. Describe what it is and why it is in the portfolio.

Step 4: Write a short reflection for each item and place it below the description or caption. The reflection explains what you learned from teaching this, what you would do differently, or something that is an insight for you that relates to this photo or lesson.

Step 5: Lay the artifact, description, and reflection on a page under a TITLE that clearly identifies the message to the reader. If the new teacher is organizing the portfolio by INTASC standards, perhaps the standard is part of the title.

Step 6: Put all the pages together. Place the Philosophy Statement up front and write a Final Statement for the last page. This Final Statement could include what I learned this year as a first-year teacher, my goals for year 2, and my future aspirations as an educator.

New Teacher Needs

Review the Plan page in the beginning of this chapter, "What is needed and wanted?" by your new teachers. Create your own Activity for a discussion topic and set aside time to address this issue with your new teachers.

What is needed by your new teachers that was not included in the Activities list for this month?

The end of the year is approaching. What will the new teachers need to know and be able to do to successfully end the school year? Often mentoring programs gear new teachers up for opening school but don't take the time to assist the new teachers in ending the school year.

How can you assist the new teachers with whom you are working to "survive" closing a classroom and closing out the school year? What would your Closing the School Year Survival Packet look like?

● REFLECT *on This Month's Discussions*

Mentor's Reflections

Directions: Complete as many of the bubble prompts as you would like after you have finished the Activites in the chapter and before you Set Goals. Add your own prompts to blank bubbles if these prompts do not meet your needs. Ask your new teachers to complete their own reflection bubbles on the next page. Compare and share your reflections at one of your meetings. You may consider using one or two reflection bubbles as topics for future mentoring discussions.

I can help the new teachers by . . .
One assumption I made this year is . . .
I see __________ differently now because . . .
An idea I would like to share before the end of the year is . . .

New Teachers' Reflections

Directions: Complete as many of the bubble prompts as you would like after you have finished the Activites in the chapter and before you Set Goals. Add your own prompts to blank bubbles if the prompts listed do not meet your needs. Compare and share your reflections with your mentor and other new teachers at a scheduled meeting.

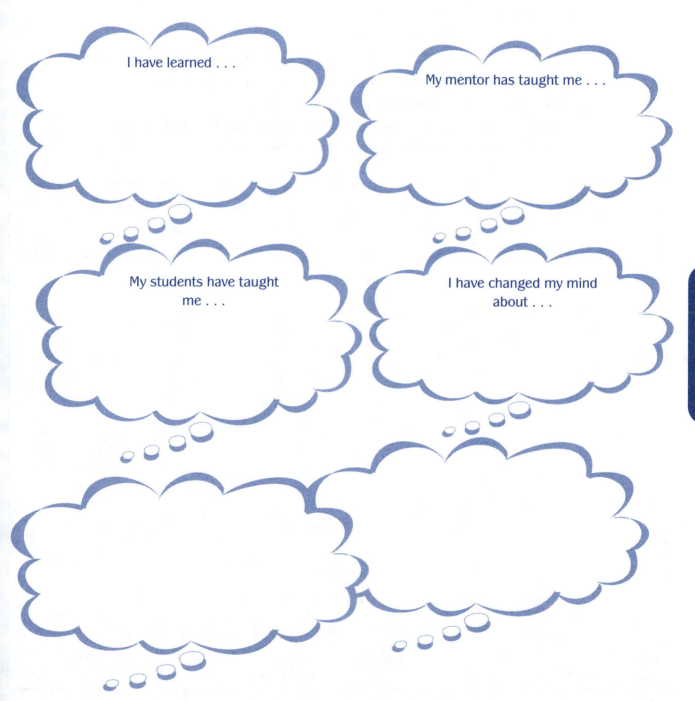

I have learned . . .

My mentor has taught me . . .

My students have taught me . . .

I have changed my mind about . . .

SET GOALS *for Next Month*

Directions:

- Complete this Set Goals page the last day of the month after your Reflection and use it to guide the first week meeting for next month.
- Review the PLAN–CONNECT–ACT pages you completed in this chapter to see what you need to revisit next month based on the new teachers' needs. List two needs that stand out for you right now.
- Ask yourself how you would like to share what the new teachers need with them.

  Will you give a tour of your classroom?

  Will you share materials you have made?

  Will you take them to the library and show them how to use existing resources?

  Will you connect them with people who can assist them regularly?

  What will you do to be an effective mentor?
- List two goals for yourself as a mentor for next month. How do your goals relate to what observe the new teachers' top two needs to be?

New Teacher Needs (from reflections, conversations, and your observations)	**Your Mentor Goals**
1.	1.
2.	2.

A good teacher adds some humor to teaching. —Seventh-Grade Student

Completing the Year

Paperwork, Relationships, and Closing a Room

New Teacher Phase: Celebrate, Culminate, and Reflect

"I felt like I was racing to get everything done for the last day, and the next day everyone was gone! No students, no directives from the central office, just me feeling exhausted and exhilarated. I did it! I finished! Now I know what I will do differently next year!"

INTASC Principles

Revisit INTASC Principle 9.

- **PRINCIPLE 9 Professional Growth/Reflection**
  The teacher is a reflective practitioner who continually evaluates the effects of his or her choices and actions on others (students, parents, and other professionals in the learning community) and who actively seeks out opportunities to grow professionally.

Completing the Year

Paperwork, Relationships, and Closing a Room

This is the time to celebrate, culminate the year, and reflect on what happened. It has been a whirlwind for the new teachers and for you as well. It is not over yet, because the cleanup and closing down take lots of time and energy too. Keep the new teachers upbeat as they move through the last month. Use your sense of humor with them and take time to remind them of the humorous things that have happened all year.

This chapter focuses on nuts and bolts like cleanup and also the more serious side of looking at what actually happened this year. Continue to meet with the new teachers this month because they will have lots of questions. Just like the orientation in August, the ending of the year brings so many little details. Where do these books get stored? Who gets the report cards? How do I lock up and clean up my room? You have done this so many times it is second nature. Remember it is not for the new teachers. Perhaps you may want to create a closing the year Survival Kit. Be sure to put some fun items in the kit for the teachers!

Use the activities in this chapter to discover what the new teachers are feeling right now. Make time for meetings even though the schedules seem packed with other duties. This is the time to reap the ideas that the new teachers have been thinking about all year. This is when the harvest of work is complete. Videotaping the classrooms for them is a nice way of documenting what their first classroom looked like and how they set it up. It also is a reminder to them for next year when they want to make changes. Your letter to the new teachers doesn't have to be long, and you don't have to give it to them in June. You may want to wait and reflect on what you would like to say and send it off in July or August. You know they will appreciate your words.

Your year as a mentor is coming to a close. Review your original writing in August and see how far you have come in your thinking and learning. What were the surprises in the role? What did you enjoy? What was difficult for you? Will you ever mentor again?

Acknowledge yourself for doing this work and go out with other mentors to celebrate your accomplishments in preparing the next generation of teachers. Bravo!

What Do We Want to Talk about When We Meet This Month?

Invite your new teachers to write down a short list of questions and bring them to your first June meeting. Use the questions below as a guide for your discussions throughout the month.

New Teachers' Possible Questions:

1. I need help in closing up my room. What should I do first?
2. How should I reflect on my year? Will you meet with me?
3. Should I seek feedback from others (students, parents, colleagues, etc.) to gain insights into my year?
4. Do you have any final words of advice as I complete my first year?

List the other questions your new teachers brought to the meeting so you will have them for your next mentoring cycle.

As a Mentor, You Can Ask Questions, Too!

Try to ask more questions to learn about your new teachers, rather than telling them how things should be done.

Mentor's Possible Questions:

1. What did you learn about yourself as a teacher this year?
2. What did you learn about your students and their families this year?
3. How can I help you complete the year and do your June closing work?
4. What can I do to assist you right now that would reduce your anxiety?

● PLAN *Agendas and Schedule Meetings*

Plan your monthly meetings, decide when and how you want to Connect with each other as well as others in the school and community, select the Activities from this chapter that make sense for you to discuss, Reflect separately at the end of the end of the month and share your reflection, and Set Goals for next year.

PLAN *Agendas for Monthly Meetings Based on New Teacher Needs*

Planning quality conversations means that the needs of the new teacher must be met. Take time to complete the chart before making decisions about what you will discuss at your monthly mentoring sessions. What makes most sense for you as a mentor to share in June?

Complete this together and save for future discussion. Make a copy for the new teacher if needed.

What is needed and wanted in June?

New Teacher *I need . . .*	Mentor *I want to share . . .*

When Will We Meet?

Plan to meet at times that allow you to have quality time together without interruptions. Knowing when you will meet reduces anxiety for both of you all month. New teachers look forward to planned meetings.

When will you meet?

How many times during the month?

How long will you meet for quality conversations? Ten, twenty, or thirty minutes? Indicate that on this calendar.

Will your new teacher observe you teach and demonstrate a skill this month?

Will you observe the new teachers this month? Purpose of the observation is . . .

Are there other teachers or community members your new teachers need to connect with this month? Indicate on this schedule.

Make a copy of this calendar for each new teacher. Also put these times into your teaching plan book.

June Calendar

MONDAY	TUESDAY	WEDNESDAY	THURSDAY	FRIDAY

Key: B = before school D = during the day (preparation time or lunch time) A = After school

• CONNECT *with People, Readings, Professional Associations, Resources, and Technology*

What resources exist in your school and community that could assist new teachers in completing the year?

Directions:

1. Review the answers you both completed in the "What is needed and wanted?" boxes on page 242. What does the new teacher need? What do you want to share? Keep the answers to these questions in mind when you explore possible resources.
2. Copy this Connect page so you both can investigate resources separately. Bring your completed June Plan and Connect pages to the June meeting. Plan together how you will close out the school year.

CONNECT *with People . . .*

Who in the school building (experienced teachers, other beginning teachers, custodians, secretaries, etc.) may be able to help with June needs?

Who in the community can assist in ending the school year?

How can parents be helpful in reflecting on your first year?

CONNECT *with Readings, Professional Associations, and Resources . . .*

What have you read or used that would assist ending a school year? New teachers may refer to student teaching courses and readings. Mentors will have protocols and materials that relate to this topic.

CONNECT *with Technology . . .*

Find websites and links that will provide information about:

- The last week of school
- Reflection and writing about practice
- Beginning the second year
- Professional development opportunities

● ACTIVITIES: *Select Topics for Quality Discussions*

What Will We Discuss at Our June Meetings?

Each month begins with a formal first week planning meeting where dates and times for discussions are scheduled. Use the agenda in this chapter to guide your meeting. Select Activity pages listed on this page as possible talking points at this meeting or for any other meetings you schedule during the month. Record your meeting dates and time on your Planning Calendar. You may decide to assign some Activity pages to the new teacher for completion alone. Use the Appendix for five-, ten-, fifteen-, twenty-, thirty-, and sixty-minute meeting formats you may want to use during the month.

Schedule this meeting during the first week of the month	**PLAN the Monthly Discussions (see sample agenda)**
✓ The Activities you will discuss	**ACT by Selecting Appropriate Topics for Discussions during the Month**
	Activities for June discussions related to *Completing the Year* include . . .
	ACT 1 Closing Procedures and Paperwork
	ACT 2 Videotaping
	ACT 3 Letter to Myself
	ACT 4 Letter to Future First-Year Teachers
	ACT 5 Letter to Students and Parents
	ACT 6 Letter to Mentor
	* ACT 7 Classroom and Behavior Management Issues
	* ACT 8 Looking at Student Work
	* ACT 9 Communicating with Parents
	* ACT 10 Observing New Teachers
	* ACT 11 Preparing a Professional Portfolio: Table of Contents
	ACT 12 Sharing the Professional Portfolio
	ACT 13 New Teacher Needs
The last day of the month the new teachers and you complete these pages on your own.	**REFLECT and SET GOALS for Next Year** **Give new teachers copies of REFLECT and SET GOALS pages for next year.**

*These five Activities will be offered each month from January through June.

June

● *First Week Agenda: Making a Plan for the Month*

TOPIC: Completing the Year: Paperwork, Relationships, and Closing a Room

Have snacks and water or soft drinks available. Hold the meeting in your classroom or another comfortable space where you will be sure you will not be interrupted. Put a colorful sign on your door that says "Mentoring Meeting—Please do not disturb."

First: Welcome and introductions: Invite new teachers to share something that is going well.

Then: Review the May new teacher Reflections.

- How did the new teachers respond? How will this impact what you do next?
- Share any of your mentor Reflections that are appropriate.

Next: Review the Set Goals page that you both completed the last day of May.

- How will these goals carry over into this month?
- What do we want to talk about when we meet this month?
- Share the possible key questions listed at the beginning of this chapter.
- What most interests the new teachers right now?

Begin: Plan what you will discuss this month use the Planning calendar to set your meeting times. Think about how you should share information with the new teachers. Will you give handouts, a tour of your room, or hold discussions? Review the Activities pages for handouts and discussion ideas. Use the Appendix for five-, ten-, fifteen-, twenty-, thirty-, and sixty-minute meeting templates. Modify Activities and templates as needed.

Network: Complete the Connections page together.

Acknowledge: Recognize what you and the new teachers have done so far instead of focusing on what they don't know. Remind the new teachers that they will complete Reflections and Set Goals for next year.

Share: End the session with compliments for each new teacher and at least one practical idea related to closing a school year. Let new teachers share ideas, too.

Closing Procedures and Paperwork

Discuss in detail how the new teacher should close the classroom and what must be handed in to the office the last day of school. Very often teacher induction programs do a great job of orienting new teachers to the school but forget how to end the year. There are cultural norms in schools for doing certain things certain ways. This doesn't mean the new teachers shouldn't question things and try to make them better, it just means you as a mentor need to tell them what the school culture is and why it is that way.

Possible paperwork:

Grades for students by a certain dates

Promotion cards or paperwork for retaining students

Report cards for principal review a week before students get them

Special needs student reports and IEPs

Other . . .

Closing the room may involve:

Covering all the shelves with paper

Removing all the books

Putting things in storage

Washing and cleaning furniture

Other . . .

New teachers could use students to assist them in some of these closing procedures if they know what they are in advance. Often what happens is that new teachers don't know what is expected, and they are left washing all the desks the day after the students are dismissed. Assist your new teachers so they can benefit from your knowledge about closing the school year.

Videotaping

It is not too late to have the new teacher videotape himself or herself teaching a lesson. In fact, this may be the perfect time! The end of the year is when the new teacher may have more confidence with the curriculum and experience in managing the classroom.

Suggestions for videotaping include:

1. Tell the new teachers to focus the camera on the students, not themselves. This way they can see the impact of their teaching on the students rather than their "teaching performance." This puts the new teachers more at ease because they don't have to watch themselves on camera! It also allows them to see their students in action—especially those students they may not be watching when they are giving directions.
2. Make sure all proper permissions slips for videotaping are completed.
3. Encourage the new teacher to list two or three things he or she would like to view in the tape.
4. Observe the videotape together if possible. Discuss what is going on. Stop the tape at certain places and ask the new teacher what he or she notices or why he or she thinks this student is performing a certain way. Look at the two or three issues the new teacher highlighted.
5. Ask the new teacher if there is anything else he or she noticed in the tape.

Using videotape to create a class documentary

Let the students get involved to create an end of the year message for the new teacher!

Using videotape to record the room arrangement and bulletin boards

Scan the room to record how things were set up and projects that were on the boards or students' work.

Think of other ways you could encourage new teachers to use videotape.

A Letter to Myself

Encourage the new teachers to write a journal entry or a letter to themselves at the end of the year. They don't have to share it with anyone.

The last day of school

Dear Self,

This has been a year full of surprises and challenges. Some of them have been…

I have learned . . .

I feel good about . . . Personally I appreciate the way I was able to . . .

I see myself . . . next year. I really enjoyed . . .

I am confident that . . . The best thing about being a first year teacher was . . .

I am looking forward to next year because . . .

Sincerely,

A Letter to Future First-Year Teachers

Prepare an open letter to next year's first-year teachers. Type the letter so that your letter can be copied and shared or placed in a binder for prospective new teachers to read. New teachers listen to other new teachers. This letter is a way of leaving a legacy to future teachers.

Date: ________________

Dear New Teacher,

I have just completed my first year, and I have some advice for you as you begin preparing yourself for your first class.

____

____

____

____

____

____

____

____

____

____

I have also attached two of my favorite lesson plans and an article that I found to be helpful.

Sincerely,

Grade Level

If you are willing to talk to prospective student teachers, leave your email or phone number so you can be contacted. You will be a second-year teacher.

A Letter to Students and Parents

At the beginning of the year, the new teachers wrote letters to the parents (see September ACT 10). Some new teachers may also have written letters to the students, too! Encourage the new teachers to write a closing letter at the end of the year.

Letter to Students

This open letter could thank the students for their cooperation. High school students would value this type of communication. It could acknowledge the work they did during the school year or highlight special activities. It does not have to be long, but it does have to be specific and authentic. Discuss ways new teachers could include specifics without having to state every student's name. How could the new teacher use humor? How could this be personalized? Perhaps one sentence could be written at the bottom of each letter to that student? How is this different from the comments on the report card?

Other ideas for student letters could be:

Letter to the Parents

This open letter could refer to the original letter written in the fall. For most new teachers this will seem like a long time ago. Brainstorm what parents would want to hear in a letter. Would they care to hear information that is not about their own child? How could this letter be used to advance the new teacher's standing in the community? Why is this a good idea? What are the down sides to sending a letter like this? If the new teacher is using a website, the letter could be posted there.

Other ideas for parent letters could be:

A Letter to the Mentor

This is an opportunity for you to receive feedback from your new teachers. Make a list of questions you would like the new teachers to cover in a letter format. It is an important way to close the year and wind down the formal relationship you have had all year. Assign this well after the close of the year so the new teachers will be honest with you. This information can serve as an evaluation for you as you work with new teachers in the future.

Possible topics to include in the letter . . .

Mentor's strengths
What I wish the mentor would do differently
How the mentor helped me

Add your own questions to the assignment so you will get the feedback you need to grow as a mentor.

Dear Mentor,

I appreciated . . .

Sincerely,

New Teacher

Date

Classroom and Behavior Management Issues

The year is coming to a close. One last month, and it could be the most difficult. New teachers don't know what to expect, and students are anxious to get out of school. Review all the Classroom and Behavior Management pages in this book with the new teachers.

Which ones really worked for them?

Which ones did not and why?

Discuss how the new teachers will finish off the year with their students.

Have them start thinking about what they will do next year.

What did you notice about your mentoring around this topic? How would you do it differently?

Looking at Student Work

Review Four Major Components of Differentiating Instruction

As the school year comes to a close, it is important for new teachers to stay on course and continue to modify and differentiate instruction. Sometimes this is when the new teachers drop the ball and throw in the towel. They give up. They have tried the approaches during the year, they have attended the workshops, they have integrated some pieces, but they have just gotten tired. Teaching and managing a classroom are hard enough. Even experienced teachers find it difficult to find the time to analyze, sort, see what students need next, see what they need to do, and give each student a compliment. Coach your new teachers to do what they can, even if it is just one of the components below. Time is always a factor in a teacher's day (or any teacher's day), and new teachers also have varying skill abilities in teaching, so looking at student work, although crucial, may not be the one next skill they need right now.

When getting ready to teach a new unit, discuss the ways new teachers can think about the following:

I. *Tapping into Students' Prior Knowledge*

New teachers can pretest or interview students in a variety of ways to find out what they already know. Sorting students into categories Know, Want to Know, and Learn (KWL) allows the teacher to assess the class's knowledge base. This is also an opportunity to find out who exceeds standards in the classroom on this topic.

II. *Content Knowledge*

New teachers can use varied reading levels for the same content as well as movies, CDs, and other interesting materials. Limiting vocabulary or adding enrichment words will provide the learners above or below standard with material.

III. *The Instructional Method*

New teachers need to continue to vary the way in which they deliver content. Grouping, products and process assignments, graphic organizers, and varied strategies keep students engaged as well as respond to various learning needs.

IV. *Varied Assessments*

New teachers need to use a varied of tools to assess student progress. Quizzes and tests are only one way. Remind new teachers at the end of the year to continue to measure progress in multiple ways. This will ensure that new teachers will be able to more accurately judge end of the year progress outside of the "standardized tests" mandates. Knowing what students can do and being able to communicate that to them can make the difference in their staying in school.

Communicating with Parents

A Year Ending Report to Parents

The end of the year is a hectic and incredibly exhausting time for any teacher. The new teachers are especially overwhelmed because they have never done this before. They may have to hold a student back or give a report card that is less than satisfactory. Parents may or may not have been as cooperative as the new teacher may have liked, and as a mentor you can assist the new teacher in sorting this out in a productive way. In spite of all, of this it is a time to celebrate the completion of a year and acknowledge what has been done successfully.

The final report cards will focus on the academic work, which is very important. However, there is an opportunity for the new teachers to also write a final note to parents that relates to the community of learners that developed in the classroom this year. Just as in the beginning of the year the new teacher wrote a letter of introduction, it is important at the end of the year to write some kind of closing note to parents and students. This is the new teacher's first year of teaching, and it is important to take the time to reflect on what went well and to share that with parents and students.

Brainstorm ways your new teachers could possibly do this. A website with photos from the year? An email to all students and parents thanking them for a great year? A final newsletter?

List other ideas:

Discuss why it is important to end the year with this parent communication even though the student is moving on to another grade.

Share samples of end of the year letters you may have used in the past.

When should this final communication be sent?

Celebrate and acknowledge what your new teachers have done!

Observing the New Teachers

Write a letter to the new teachers highlighting their growth and acknowledging their work with you this year. What did you observe about your new teachers?

Use the INASC standards as a guide for your letter as well as the topics below.

Personal growth
Professional growth
Teaching ability
Interaction with colleagues

You could write a general letter for all new teachers and personalize the last paragraph. Let them know how much you have gained from this experience, too. Acknowledge their expertise in the areas they have brought to the profession.

What do you want to say about each new teacher?

	Specific Highlights
New teacher #1	
New teacher #2	
New teacher #3	
New teacher #4	

Preparing a Professional Portfolio: Table of Contents

____ *Philosophy Statement* (one page)

____ *Professional Profile* (third person; one paragraph)

Highlight your professionalism, additional activities, and strengths by including a professional profile in the portfolio. Like a biography, this narrative will provide your readers with highlights of your best features: languages you speak, places you have traveled, sports you play or coach, and skills you bring to teaching. Review your student teaching profile and résumé for ideas. Use an author's description on a book jacket to guide you.

____ *Instructional Practice*

This will be the major portion of your portfolio. It should be organized by competencies and/or themes with reflections and descriptions.

____ artifacts (photos, lesson plans, etc.)

____ diagrams

____ audio and video with written explanation of what is on the tape

____ samples of student work

____ *Appreciation Notes, Public Appreciation* (from parents, teachers, students)

If you saved notes people wrote to you that were positive, include them on a page titled Appreciation. If they relate to a lesson, you may include them on that page.

____ *Evaluation Reports* (from supervisor and cooperating teacher)

____ *Guest Register* (last page)

This page is for people to sign and date when they read it. Space for one brief comment should be included.

Optional

Create your own teaching trifold brochure highlighting your skills, goals, and attributes. Design it like a business brochure to be shared with parents.

Sharing the Professional Portfolio

Host a portfolio sharing party with all the new teachers. Get together with other mentors and plan a social event that brings everyone together. Design a Guest Register page that will allow readers to sign it and make a brief comment. Have food, music, and place the portfolios on a table where guests can flip though and sign the guest register. If time allows, videotape each new teacher with his or her portfolio. Let each person show just one page and have each one share one thing he or she learned by completing this portfolio.

Encourage the new teachers to share the portfolio next year with . . .

the principal or department chair
the school committee
faculty at the school
parents at an open house in the fall
students the first day of school of the second year
new students who come in later in the year
community business partners

Think of other ways the new teachers can share their work.

New Teacher Needs

Review the Plan page in the beginning of this chapter, "What is needed and wanted?" by your new teachers. Create your own Activity for a discussion topic and set aside time to address this issue with your new teachers.

What is needed by your new teachers that was not included in the Activities list for this month?

How can you help the new teacher in this area?

June is typically the ending of the school year in most parts of the country. What do the new teachers need to do at the end of the school year? If you created a Closing the School Year Survival Packet in May, take the time to discuss it now. Did it help the new teachers? What will you add next time?

• REFLECT *on This Month's Discussions*

Mentor's Reflections

Directions: Reread all the Reflections you completed from August through May. Then complete all of the bubble prompts below. Share your responses with your mentor coordinator or other supportive administrator to improve the program.

Ask your new teachers to complete their own reflection bubbles on the next page and to bring them to your final meeting. Combine all the responses and anonymously share them with your mentor coordinator or supportive administrator so the new teachers' voices will be heard.

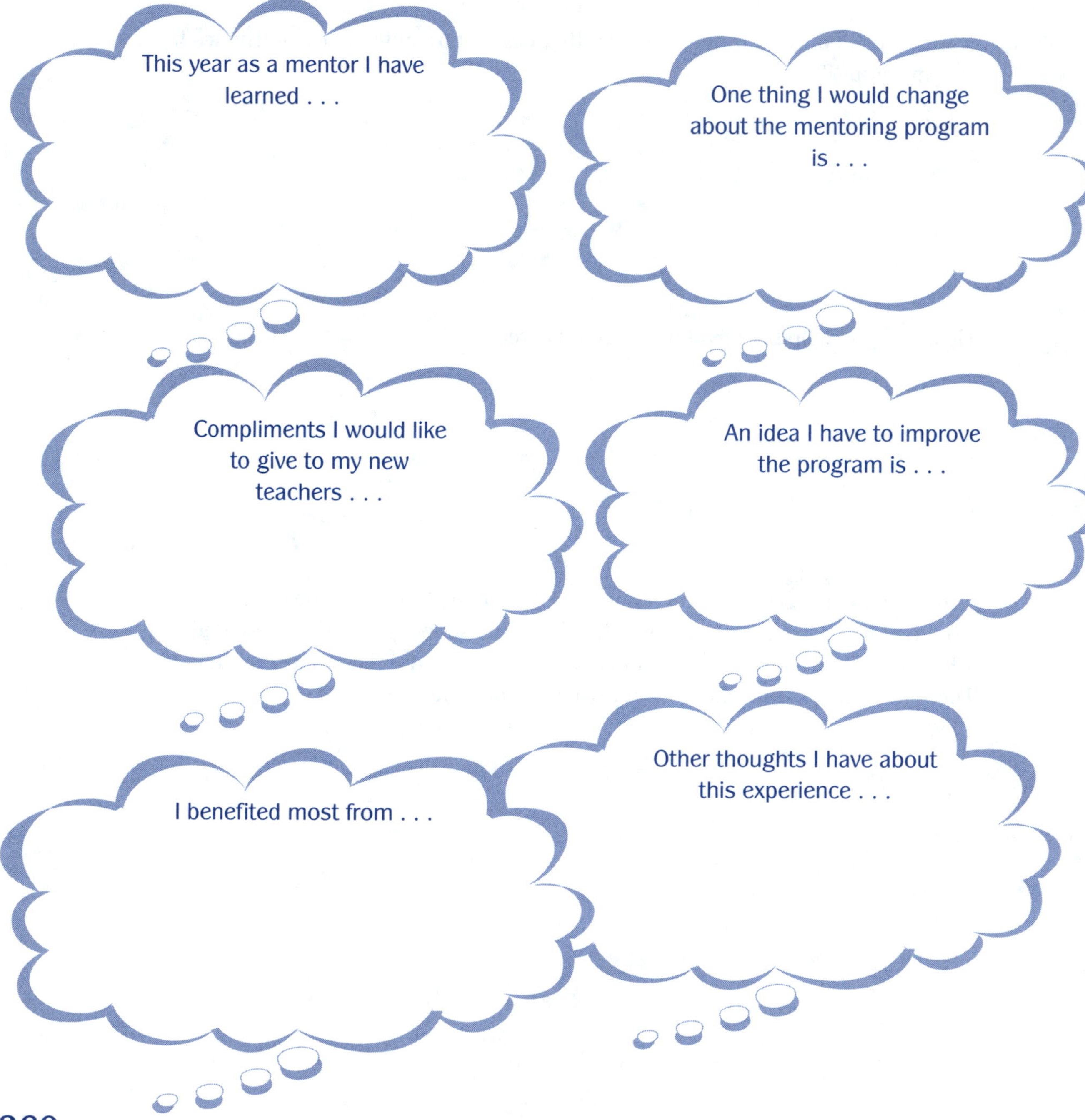

This year as a mentor I have learned . . .
One thing I would change about the mentoring program is . . .
Compliments I would like to give to my new teachers . . .
An idea I have to improve the program is . . .
I benefited most from . . .
Other thoughts I have about this experience . . .

New Teachers' Reflections

Directions: Reread all the Reflections you completed from August through May. Then complete all of the bubble prompts below. Share your responses with your mentor to improve the program.

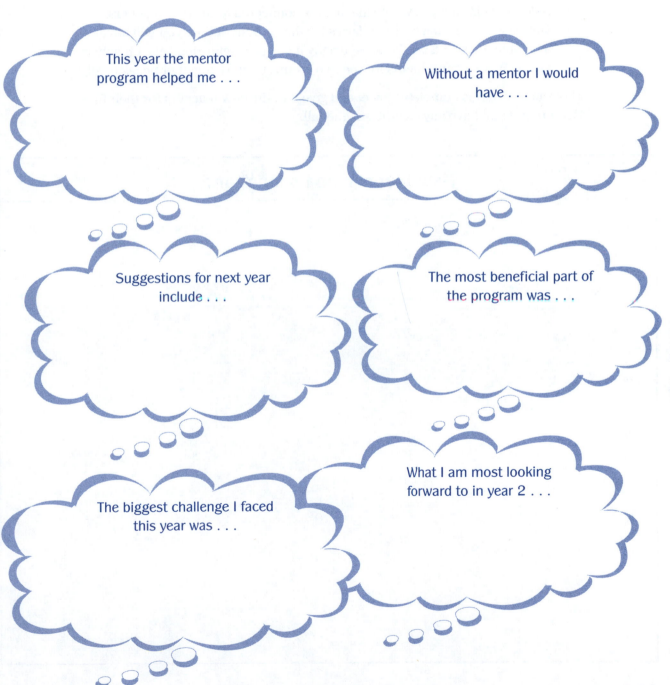

This year the mentor program helped me . . .

Without a mentor I would have . . .

Suggestions for next year include . . .

The most beneficial part of the program was . . .

The biggest challenge I faced this year was . . .

What I am most looking forward to in year 2 . . .

● SET GOALS *for Next Year*

Directions:

- Review the PLAN–CONNECT–ACT pages you completed this year to see what you think the new teachers need to focus on in Year 2.
- Ask the new teachers what they think they would like to focus on in Year 2. Compare their list to yours and agree on three goals. Write them on this Set Goals sheet.
- If Year 2 teachers do not have mentors, brainstorm ways the new teachers could support each other in their second year.
- Ask yourself how you would like to stay connected to the new teachers. Define your role and set boundaries for the amount of time you will have available for Year 2 teachers, especially if you are mentoring Year 1 teachers again. Make arrangements for the two groups to work together occasionally.

Make a copy of this completed sheet and give it to the new teachers for their files. Refer to it if you have any meetings in the fall.

New Teacher Goals for Year 2
1.
2.
3.

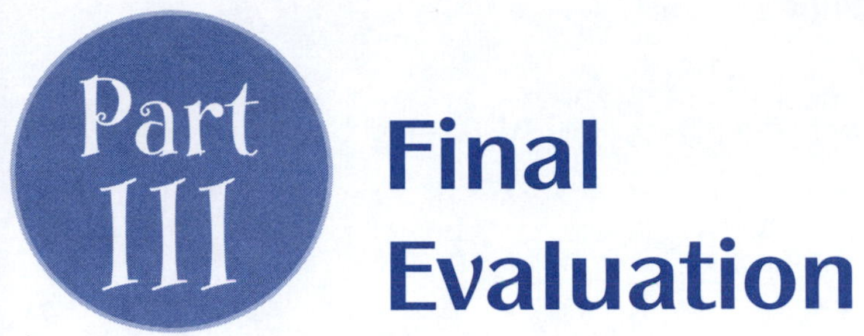

Final Evaluation

At the end of the school year when you have completed the month-by-month mentoring curriculum, you should take some time to evaluate how this systematic discussion worked for you and your new teachers. If you offered this program as a course for credit, you may need some documentation for district administrators. What will that be? Perhaps samples of Activities pages or Reflections?

What Have You Learned?

Ask yourself . . .

- Would I mentor again? Why or why not?
- How will I use this curriculum next time?
- What is the most significant thing I learned this year?
- What am I most grateful for in this process?
- How will I share what I have learned with the district administrators and induction coordinators?

Next Steps

- What one step could I take right now that would advance this mentoring work?
- What do I wish for around the induction and mentoring work in my school? My district?
- What were the "plusses" of participating in this program?

Appendix

Mentor Templates for Quality Conversations with New Teachers

You have been assigned to a new teacher.
You have never been a mentor before.
You ask yourself, "What are we supposed to talk about and how can I fit these conversations into my day?"

Ideas illustrating what you can discuss with one new teacher in five, ten, fifteen, twenty, thirty, sixty, or 120 minutes to advance teaching and learning are listed.

Short, Informal, Unplanned, Public Meetings

Sometimes you will see your new teacher in passing. It might be in the hallway, the lunchroom, or before or after school. What can you do or say when you only have five, ten, or fifteen minutes that are unplanned and in a public place?

A: The Five-Minute Meeting: *Giving an Authentic Compliment*

B: The Ten-Minute Meeting: *Sharing an Idea or Resource*

C: The Fifteen-Minute Meeting: *Problem to Possibilities*

Longer, Scheduled or Unscheduled Meetings

Sometimes you will find yourself sharing a preparation period together that was not scheduled on your Plan calendar. You can use this extended time together in a productive way. D through F provide some options that would focus your discussion during this typically unscheduled time. You may also want to use these templates as part of your regular monthly discussions. The five-, ten-, and fifteen-minute templates are also topic options during these longer meeting times.

D: The Twenty-Minute Meeting: *What's Working? How Do You Know?*

E: The Thirty-Minute Meeting: *Looking at Student Work Together*

F: The Sixty-Minute Meeting: *Observing the Mentor*

Sample Integrated Sixty-Minute Meeting

G: The Integrated Meeting: *Focus on Student Learning*

Teacher Research—120 Minutes with Followup Meetings

H: Inquiry into Practice: *Finding a Question and Finding the Answers*

A. The Five-Minute Meeting: *Giving an Authentic Compliment*

You are rushing to class and you see your new teacher standing by his door. You know you only have five minutes. What can you say? Try giving a compliment. Think about what you have been talking about in your other meetings. What have you noticed about the new teacher? If you have visited his classroom, what have you noticed? What are you noticing right now?

As with your own students, you know that unsubstantiated praise does not work. Just saying "I think you are doing a great job" sometimes confuses students and new teachers. Because both students and new teachers want to "do it right," they do want some praise or feedback. If you give nonspecific praise, new teachers may be asking themselves, "What am I actually doing that deserves this praise?" Mostly because they want to replicate it to get more praise! If they don't know what "it" is they may not be able to repeat the behavior. The key to compliments is to be specific and authentic. Don't just give a compliment because you think you have to say something.

Some sample compliments could be:

> *I noticed the way you were talking to that student. You made eye contact, you lowered your voice, you kept a professional stance, and it looks like you got the results you wanted. Good job!*
>
> *The bulletin boards in your room are really engaging. I like the way you made them interactive so students who finish their work can go up and complete an activity. Good idea!*
>
> *The lesson plan you shared at our last meeting was very thoughtful and clearly written. I especially liked the way you tied the district goals to the learning activity. Nicely done!*

Compliments can also be integrated into all of your meetings. Everyone likes a compliment. Remember to give a few to yourself. Mentors need compliments, too! Try saying this:

> *I like the way I am focusing my time with the new teachers. By planning what I am going to talk about I seem to get more done and it is fitting into my day. I like mentoring!*

B. The Ten-Minute Meeting: *Sharing an Idea or Resource*

You meet your new teacher in line at the copy machine at morning break. Rather than making small talk, use this time productively to share an idea that has been working in your room. If your new teacher is not in your subject area or grade level, adapt the idea on the spot to show how many ideas can be used across grade levels and content area.

Sample ideas for sharing:

> *I just tried this history lesson in my classroom. I had the students taking notes during my lecture, and I gave them a worksheet that had some of the notes printed. They had to listen to me and fill in the blanks as they went. It really made them pay attention and it also helped some of my students who are having difficulty copying everything. How do you think this might fit in your English class?*
>
> *I just got these manipulatives out of the library. It looks like they are new. I used them and the kids really stayed engaged. I know you are third grade, but I think your students would like them, too. How do you think they would fit into your curriculum?*

Be sure that your sharing idea ends with a question so the new teacher has to think about how to use the resource. Have it be OK for the new teacher to say no, too. Every idea is not a good or useful one at the time. The key is the sharing part and that you are open to consistently throwing ideas the new teacher's way.

You can also share the names of people, places, and other Connections as they come up. New teachers want and need to be networked. Think purposefully and systematically about how you are doing this.

C. The Fifteen-Minute Meeting: *Problem to Possibilities*

You see the new teacher in the library and you both share that you have 15 minutes to talk. The new teacher tells you she is still having trouble with one student who is unmotivated in her classroom.

Complete these questions with the new teacher:

1. Identify the problem: What is the student actually doing? Saying? Not doing?

2. What has the new teacher already tried? Talking to the students? The parents? The administration? The school counselor?

3. Brainstorm several possible solutions to this problem with the new teacher.

   Possibility A:

   Possibility B:

   Possibility C:

4. Ask the new teacher to summarize the meeting and state what his next steps will be.

5. The next time you talk check it to see if any possibilities worked. If not, create three more.

Let the new teacher know that every problem cannot be solved quickly, and you may need to do this problem solving more than once. Avoid telling the new teacher how you would solve the problem. One possible option could be yours, but be sure the new teacher feels empowered to implement the option of her choice. She may have to try all three!

D. The Twenty-Minute Meeting: *What's Working? How Do You Know?*

Ask your new teacher to list five things that are working for him. Discuss how he knows they are working. The purpose of this discussion is to actually encourage the new teacher (with you) to look at the "evidence" that demonstrates what is going smoothly.

You could also do this process in reverse. What is NOT working? How do you know? Then you could complete a Problem to Possibilities process to brainstorm options for making the situation work.

Examples of what might be working for an elementary teacher:

What's Working?	How Do You Know?
1. My students are on time for class.	I take attendance and they are here.
2. I taught a great science lesson today.	The students were engaged, I had no discipline problems, and they passed the quiz at the end of the class.
3. My students were well behaved in music.	The music teacher gave them a compliment.
4. I integrated my new student who doesn't speak English into the classroom successfully.	I gave her a partner and they played together and worked together all day.
5. I made time for myself last night at home.	I didn't bring any schoolwork home, instead I did some exercise and read a personal book. I feel great today.

Complete this table with your new teacher. You could also use this process with a group of new teachers as part of one of your monthly meetings.

What's Working?	How Do You Know?

E. The Thirty-Minute Meeting: *Looking at Student Work Together*

You have a preparation period and you area able to visit your new teacher's classroom—or it is the end of the day and you have thirty minutes to spare. What can you do?

Ask the new teacher to select some student work that you can look at together. If your district has a rubric, use that to analyze the student work. Design a rubric if there is not one available.

1. Skim through a set of papers:

   Select student achieved the goal of the lesson.

   Select one paper that may have met the goal.

   Select one that looks like the student did not achieve the goal.

2. Read the papers together and decide where they fit on the rubric. You may each do it separately and compare your ratings. Were you similar in your rubric rating?

3. Take it a step further: Take one paper and together analyze it for the following:

   What can we compliment this student for in this paper?

   What is the next learning step for this student?

   What *one* thing should I focus on with this student?

4. Do this for the other two papers you selected.

   What did you learn from doing this process?

   Talk about the process of looking at student work with your new teacher and how it informs the teacher's practice. Discuss ways to differentiate curriculum to meet the needs of diverse learners.

F. The Sixty-Minute Meeting: *Observing the Mentor*

Your new teachers can learn a lot by watching you teach. Demonstration lessons on one particular topic or content discipline can provide a focus for many discussions. A successful demonstration lesson should be scheduled when you have time before and after the lesson to talk with the new teachers. Inviting two or more teachers into your room at the same time allows them to discuss what they see together, and it further informs their observation of successful practice.

Preobservation: Before the new teachers come to class, share the lesson plan and the purpose of this demonstration lesson. Why are you doing this? How will it help the new teachers? Be explicit in sharing these outcomes. Decide what the new teachers should be focusing on during the lesson and how they will record what they see. If you have more than one new teacher observing, you may assign different focus areas to them. At postobservation they can share and compare.

Observation: (see observation form on next page) Possible focus areas for observing could include how the teacher manages the classroom, what instructional strategies are used, how the classroom environment is organized, how the lesson is implemented, modifications for diverse learners, how English language learners were handled, how the lesson is part of a larger curriculum, how the lesson was assessed, and homework or enrichment that was discussed.

Postobservation: After the lesson is taught, you must bring the new teachers together to share what they observed with you. This is the key to learning for the new teachers. This is an opportunity for them to ask you questions about what you did and why you did it that way. This lab school activity offers new teachers a safe place to analyze their own practice. They are not being observed—you are! This allows them to make connections and model effective practice in their own rooms. Now they may have an idea about what they should be doing.

● Teacher Observation Template

1. Draw a floor plan of the classroom on a separate sheet of paper. Note any key physical placement of furniture or materials that stands out for you.
2. How does the mentor manage the classroom?

   Routines?

   Rules and rewards?

   Monitoring students?

   Disruptions?

3. How does the lesson plan relate to learning outcomes?

   Objectives?

   Connections to standards?

   Outcomes?

4. How does the mentor deliver instruction?

   Engaging students at the beginning of the lesson?

   Instructional strategies used?

   Technology?

   Diverse student needs?

5. How does the teacher assess learning?

   Informal assessments?

   Formal assessment?

   Homework or enrichment?

6. How would you describe the mentor's teaching style?

Preparing for the Observation

Before you invite any new teachers to your classroom, you will want to prepare yourself. When you are observed by an administrator, you think about what you will do and say. Most teachers have the lesson planned well in advance, and they prepare their students as well. Even though this observation is not as "high stakes" as one by your principal, you still need to prepare.

Ask yourself:

1. What do I want my new teachers to gain by this observation?
2. Should I talk during the class and point out what I am doing—like an instructional demonstration—or should I just teach and let them watch? What are the benefits of either approach?
3. Which lesson should I demonstrate and why?
4. How will I know if the demonstration lesson was successful to my new teachers' learning?
5. When will I schedule the postobservation discussion? (Make sure it is the same day or the following day to capture the essence of the lesson and the new teacher's insights.)
6. After the postobservation discussion, answer this question: From doing this process I learned . . .

G. The Integrated Meeting: *Focus on Student Learning*

Agenda *	
5 minutes	Compliment from mentor for new teachers. If more than one teacher is present, let them compliment each other, too.
10 minutes	Share an idea or resource—let the new teachers share with you too!
15 minutes	Problem to possibilities—invite new teachers to share a pressing problem and take some time to brainstorm possible solutions using C. Discuss how this problem relates to student learning (or not learning).
30 minutes	Look at student work together. If there is a large group, divide into smaller ones to analyze and use the E process.

**Note:* New teachers must bring samples of student work to this meeting.

H. Teacher Research: *Inquiry into Practice— Finding a Question and Finding the Answers*

Some first-year teachers will be at a level of expertise where they can actually inquire into their own practice and discover what they are doing and how they can improve to get the results they are looking for with their students. Teacher research is one way to discover what is working or not in a systematic way. If you are interested in sharing this methodology with your new teachers, review the current resources on teacher research.

Reflecting on Practice

Encourage your new teachers to keep a journal where they can record their thoughts, assumptions, biases, insights, and new ideas. It is often difficult to maintain a daily journal, but many new teachers could do a weekly entry. You may include this process as part of your monthly meetings.

Finding a Question

When new teachers write in a journal, often the same topic or situation comes up over and over. These dilemmas or issues deserve more attention and thought. Inquiry is a process of formulating a question and systematically collecting data to reveal some answers. A sample question is, "What is the impact of guided reading on my two English language learners?" Data may be in the form of interviews, student work, observations, surveys, audio, video, and tests to show how the students are responding to this guided reading program.

Finding the Answers

After the data is collected, the new teacher needs to analyze it and see how it responds to the original question. This mini-research study does not have to be complicated. If the results show it is not working and the students are not learning, then the new teacher needs to make a case for changing the method and finding a reading program that does work.